THE DETECTIVE
IN AMERICAN FICTION,
FILM, AND TELEVISION

Recent Titles in
Contributions to the Study of Popular Culture

THE DETECTIVE IN AMERICAN FICTION, FILM, AND TELEVISION

Edited by
Jerome H. Delamater and Ruth Prigozy

Prepared under the auspices of Hofstra University

Contributions to the Study of Popular Culture,
Number 63

GREENWOOD PRESS
Westport, Connecticut • London

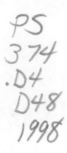

*PS
374
.D4
D48
1998*

Library of Congress Cataloging-in-Publication Data

The detective in American fiction, film, and television / edited by
    Jerome H. Delamater and Ruth Prigozy.
        p.   cm.—(Contributions to the study of popular culture,
    ISSN 0198–9871 ; no. 63)
        "Prepared under the auspices of Hofstra University."
        Includes bibliographical references and index.
        ISBN 0–313–30463–7 (alk. paper)
        1. Detective and mystery stories, American—History and criticism.
    2. Detective and mystery films—United States—History and
    criticism.   3. Detective and mystery television programs—United
    States—History and criticism.   I. Delamater, Jerome.   II. Prigozy,
    Ruth.   III. Series: Contributions to the study of popular culture ;
    no. 63.
    PS374.D4D48   1998
    813'.087209—DC21   97–1690

British Library Cataloguing in Publication Data is available.

Library of Congress Catalog Card Number: 97–1690
ISBN: 0–313–30463–7
ISSN: 0198–9871

First published in 1998

Greenwood Press, 88 Post Road West, Westport, CT 06881
An imprint of Greenwood Publishing Group, Inc.

Printed in the United States of America

The paper used in this book complies with the
Permanent Paper Standard issued by the National
Information Standards Organization (Z39.48–1984).

10 9 8 7 6 5 4 3 2 1

Copyright Acknowledgments

The editors and publisher gratefully acknowledge permission for use of the following:

Jan Whitt, "The 'Very Simplicity of the Thing': Edgar Allan Poe and the Murders He Wrote." *Clue: A Journal of Detection* 15, no. 1 (Spring/Summer 1994): 29–57. Used by permission.

Dennis Bounds, "Done to Death?: Formula and Variation in Perry Mason." In *Perry Mason: The Authorship and Reproduction of a Popular Hero*, by Dennis Bounds. Westport, CT: Greenwood Press, 1996. Greenwood Press is an imprint of Greenwood Publishing Group, Inc., Westport, CT.

Excerpts from "The Pencil" by Raymond Chandler, from *The Midnight Raymond Chandler*. Copyright © 1971 by Helga Greene, Executrix. Reprinted by permission of Houghton Mifflin Company. All rights reserved. Raymond Chandler's "The Pencil," first published in the *Daily Mail* (London)(6 April 1959), © Philip Marlowe B. V., courtesy of Ed Victor Ltd. Literary Agency, London.

To the memory of

THOMAS BELMONTE

*In honor of the 100th anniversary
of the birth of Agatha Christie,
1891–1976*

Contents

Preface

The classic British detective story is based primarily on ratiocination. Its American counterpart, however, has from the outset been described as "hard-boiled." Dashiell Hammett, Raymond Chandler, and Ross MacDonald, although approaching the genre with certainly less emphasis on the puzzle so characteristic of the British detective than on the sleuth and the criminal world, have acquired an equally formidable popular audience in both readers and filmgoers and later in television viewers. The earliest filmmakers recognized the appeal of the detective and his milieu, and the screen developed definitive versions of, for example, Sam Spade, Philip Marlowe, and Lew Archer. On television, we have become accustomed to such familiar figures as Lieutenant Columbo, Jim Rockford, and Jessica Fletcher. Ironically, this most recently developed medium has focused on figures modeled on classic British detective fiction.

In this volume, we introduce a section on the American writer Raymond Chandler and other Americans who share Chandler's approach or outlook: Elmore Leonard, Chester Himes, Faye Kellerman, Sara Paretsky, and Sue Grafton. Our second section treats film and television detectives and detection. We cannot but note that detective fiction, film, and television comprise a genre that seems constantly to reinvent itself. We look forward to whatever innovations the next century may bring.

Jerome H. Delamater
Ruth Prigozy

Acknowledgments

The editors wish to thank the Hofstra University Cultural Center for its support, encouragement, and unflagging work on behalf of the Agatha Christie interdisciplinary conference that inspired this volume. We are particularly grateful to Athelene A. Collins for her tireless efforts as conference co-ordinator. We are also appreciative of the contribution of Judy M. D'Angio, who worked so hard to prepare these essays for print.

Our editorial assistant, Kcith Dallas, has been invaluable throughout the process of preparing the volume for publication. His contribution to the preparation of scholarly references and bibliographies and his help with the myriad tasks that editors face were performed with intelligence, goodwill, and generosity of spirit. We thank him.

Finally, we wish to express our thanks to all of those others at Hofstra University who helped in this endeavor and to the university itself for creating an atmosphere in which such work can be accomplished.

THE DETECTIVE
IN AMERICAN FICTION,
FILM, AND TELEVISION

I

Raymond Chandler and American Detective Fiction

Hard-boiled detective fiction is a distinctively American subgenre, its roots traceable to nineteenth-century American isolated heroes like Natty Bumppo and other figures associated with the development of the American West. The big-city equivalent, first made popular in the 1920s by *Black Mask* magazine and in the fiction of Dashiell Hammett, is the hard-boiled detective, who has come to dominate American crime culture, reaching his apotheosis in film as Humphrey Bogart's Sam Spade (*The Maltese Falcon*) and Philip Marlowe (*The Big Sleep*). Raymond Chandler's detective, Marlowe, has exerted a particular fascination for readers, for he is more romantic than Spade while sharing the latter's elevated moral ground. He has often been described as a modern knight (as his name might suggest). And Chandler's crisp, clever metaphors, his evocation of the landscape of Los Angeles, and his penetration into hearts of darkness have influenced countless detective writers of his day and ours (Robert B. Parker is a good example of that influence).

The essays in this section concern Raymond Chandler and modern writers, male and female, who follow in his tradition. David Madden's approach to one of Chandler's most popular novels, *Farewell, My Lovely*, is a reconsideration of the author's treatment of women in his fiction. Madden focuses on Anne Riordan, comparing her appearance in the novel and in its two filmed adaptations, which in Madden's view are far less successful in their portraits of women than was Chandler in the 1940s. Steven Weisenburger's essay is a complex, theoretical discussion of Chandler's narrative form, opening up new possibilities for interpretation by examining the struggle between signs of order and error that shape all the Chandler novels. Weisenburger's essay raises provocative questions about the meaning of texts, suggesting that answers to those questions may be more elusive than solutions to the mysteries that inspired them. The third essay on Chandler is very different: James O. Tate offers a close reading of Chandler's last short story, "The Pencil." Despite the disparaging remarks of critics, Tate demonstrates that this story is as representative of Chandler's fiction as his stronger efforts and that, beneath the surface, the story is about writing, about Chandler's playing with language and the drama of composition, rather than about the mystery plot that is conventionally solved.

We have already suggested that hard-boiled detective fiction has strong connections to film, but nowhere is that connection better illustrated than in the novels of Elmore Leonard, who, as George Grella demonstrates, employs the art of cinema *in* his novels. Many of his novels are about films and filmmaking and use that medium's techniques and language to develop the narrative. Through his use of film, Grella suggests, Leonard may well belong with avant-garde artists who have extended their art in new directions.

In the novels of Chester Himes, the hard-boiled detective appears in the persons of Coffin Ed and Grave Digger, who have been the subject of considerable critical discussion involving race and Himes's portrayals of the African-American detectives. Gary Storhoff examines the critical views of Himes's fiction and, after a careful analysis, concludes that Himes defies literary conventions, structuring his work in patterns of violated expectations so that ultimately the reader is led to see the consequences of racism in America.

Diana Ben-Merre traces the Jewish detective in fiction, focusing on Harry Kemelman's Rabbi Small series and Faye Kellerman's contemporary Peter Decker novels. The essay indicates the differences between the goals of Kemelman and Kellerman, as reflected in the kinds of characters developed by each author, and demonstrates how both writers help to demystify, through Jewish-American mysteries, the Jewish character.

The final essay in this section examines the female hard-boiled detectives created by two of the most popular women writers of the genre: Sue Grafton and Sara Paretsky. Their detectives, respectively Kinsey Millhone and V. I. Warshawski, are the subjects of Timothy Shuker-Haines and Martha M. Umphrey's essay, which illustrates the differences between the male and female hard-boiled detectives and demonstrates that gender is central to both the construction of the detective and the development of the narrative. In this last essay, we can see the degree to which modernist criticism, particularly that involving gender and ideology, has recast our approach to the genre. As Ms. Umphrey remarks in her note at the end of the essay, the effect of feminist criticism of the genre may be to dissolve the very form of the detective narrative —as has this essay—into non-resolution.

1

Anne Riordan:
Raymond Chandler's Forgotten Heroine

David W. Madden

Since his death in 1959, Raymond Chandler has been elevated to detective fiction's pantheon of writers; and many scholars have even ventured to argue that Chandler's is an important voice in twentieth-century fiction, without qualifying this achievement by noting that he worked in a popular idiom. While there has been considerable discussion about many features of his writing (its style, plotting, historical verisimilitude, and the like), one area—Marlowe's and, by extension the arguments invariably seem to run, Chandler's attitudes towards women—has provoked some heated responses.

All manner of evidence has been paraded to reveal the detective-cum-author's deepest feelings, but almost always lost in the shuffle is any detailed consideration of particular female portraits. Certainly the villainesses—alluring, sexually provocative, and always deadly—have been given their due, but rarely have the other women (not necessarily the "good girls" but the less exaggerated female types) been adequately considered. One of, if not *the* most important of these is Anne Riordan, a twenty-eight-year-old woman who appears in Chandler's second novel, *Farewell, My Lovely* (1940). In this paper I intend to discuss this portrait and briefly compare it to the treatment the character receives in the two most prominent film versions of the novel—*Murder My Sweet* (1944) and *Farewell, My Lovely* (1975)[1]—to demonstrate that the "problems" Marlowe/Chandler supposedly has with women do not apply to this character. In fact, Hollywood, not Chandler, has the greater problem with the novel's women, and nowhere is this more evident than in the depictions of Anne Riordan in these two films.

It is now a tired cliché to say that Chandler wrote in a hard-boiled style and that this manner seriously colored all his human portraits. Of course it did; but Chandler, as many critics have argued, was a serious and extremely adroit writer who sought to use but not to be hamstrung by the conventions of the genre he worked within. As Chandler wrote in one letter:

the most durable thing in writing is style, and style is the most valuable investment a writer can make with his time. . . . He can't do it by trying, because the kind of style I am thinking about is a projection of personality and you have to have a personality before you can project it. ("Letter to Mrs. Robert J. Hogan, March 7, 1947," 75)

He sought a way in which to explore the complexities of human emotion and to do so in a language (albeit exaggerated) that would be immediately recognizable to a wide audience. Naturally, with such a language there come certain attitudes, which many have been quick to ascribe to Marlowe/Chandler's personality.[2]

Two of these attitudes involve misogyny and homophobia, and a pair of critics in particular have argued that Marlowe is a woman-hating homosexual. The first of these salvos was fired by Gershon Legman in *Love & Death: A Study in Censorship*, in which he asserts that Chandler's "women are all strictly flaming bitches, killers, or corpses"; he goes on to announce that "[t]he true explanation of Marlowe's temperamental disinterest in women is not 'honor,' but his interest in men. . . . Marlowe is clearly homosexual—a butterfly, as the Chinese say, dreaming that he is a man" (Legman 69-70). The first of these charges is simply preposterous, and even a cursory look at Anne Riordan, Mavis Weld in *The Little Sister*, or Linda Loring in *The Long Goodbye* should dispel this notion. The second charge, overstated like the first, may have some merit and has been framed far more carefully by another critic.[3]

In his essay "Marlowe, Men, and Women," Michael Mason develops more fully the implications of Legman's theory. Mason clearly demonstrates that Chandler often places women in the role of chief culprit and murderer and therefore concludes that the novels' "moral scheme is in truth pathologically harsh on women, and pathologically lenient towards men" (95). But victim of the same hyperbole as Legman, Mason also claims, "There is scarcely a dislikable man to be found" (95); Marlowe, he argues, is especially susceptible to "male charm" and given to provoking beatings as a masochistic "alternative to the heterosexual bond" (91).

The charge that there are scarcely any dislikable men in the novels is patently ridiculous, though perhaps Mason finds a special charm in malignant types such as Lash Canino (*The Big Sleep*), Jules Amthor and Dr. Sonderborg (*Farewell, My Lovely*), Eddie Prue (*The High Window*), Detective Moses Maglashan and Orrin Quest (*The Little Sister*), and Big Willie Magoon (*The Long Goodbye*). Furthermore, Laird Brunette, the gambling-boat operator who owns the political machinery of Bay City, is anything but one of Chandler's "engaging and kindly" villains. Under Brunette's polite, urbane exterior, there is a cold vein of iron, and Chandler's description of him is a carefully modulated study in ambiguity:

He was neither young nor old, neither fat nor thin. Spending a lot of time on or near the ocean had given him a good healthy complexion. His hair was nut-brown and waved naturally and waved still more at sea. His forehead was narrow and brainy and his eyes held a delicate menace. They were yellowish in color. He had nice hands, not babied to the point of insipidity, but well-kept. His dinner clothes were midnight blue, I judged, because they looked so black. (*Farewell, My Lovely* 224)

Indeed, Brunette is a physically attractive character; however, the color imagery in the passage offers a distinct contrast to surface appearance. Brown, yellow, and black are all colors associated with dissolution and decay; and like the "velvety tough guys" he surrounds himself with, Brunette is as tough and corrupt as they come.

For the purposes of this discussion, however, the most crucial consideration is Mason's charge that "[w]arm, erotic feeling and loving contact with a woman are irreconcilable for Marlowe" (92); the relationship with Anne Riordan appears to be a perfect case in point. Jerry Speir describes her as "one of Chandler's strongest, most independent, most likeable female characters" but leaves his assessment there (113). A closer look at her individual features reveals why she is such a distinct female portrait in Chandler's canon.

Physically she is quite attractive, though when describing her Marlowe repeatedly notices small defects—too wide a mouth, too narrow a forehead, too long an upper lip—yet he insists throughout, "It was a nice face, a face you get to like" (73). This noting of exceedingly minor imperfections emerges more as protection against attraction than any clear sign of ethical defect. In fact, Marlowe returns repeatedly to particular features of her face—her full auburn hair, teeth, shadowed and "gold-flecked eyes" (224), "neat chin" (156), and "smile [that can be] cozy and acid at the same time" (157). As Speir rightly concludes, Marlowe is definitely attracted to Riordan.

At one point though, when discussing the case with homicide Lieutenant Randall (one of Chandler's few fair cops), Marlowe declares, in response to Randall's insistence that Riordan likes him, "'I like smooth shiny girls, hardboiled and loaded with sin'" (166). Actually this is little more than macho posturing, especially when compared with his earlier remark about Anne, "You could get to like that face a lot. Glamoured up blondes were a dime a dozen, but that was a face that would wear. I smiled at it" (81).

Similarly, Marlowe finds her bungalow especially appealing with its high bookcases, comfortable chairs, warm fireplace, and with "nothing womanish ... except a full length mirror with a clear sweep of the floor in front of it" (156). Rather than misogynistic, his remark reflects something essential he finds in Riordan's nature—her straightforward, unpretentious demeanor. Marlowe is, in fact, so attracted to the place, he admits, "'A fellow could settle down here. . . . Move right in. Everything set for him'" (157).

However, the attraction goes far deeper than physical appearance or amenities, for Anne Riordan has abilities and comes from a background similar to Marlowe's and operates as a mirror image of him throughout. She is, first and foremost, a cop's daughter, her father the former honest police chief of Bay City who lost his job when Brunette's henchmen took control. Similarly, Marlowe is a former investigator for the district attorney's office who lost his job "for talking back" (106).

Like a cop, Riordan is effective in sniffing out clues, often before Marlowe can even get his bearings. She, for instance, worms information about the necklace out of the tough Randall, learns the Grayle family's connection with jade from a jeweler and a society editor, and arranges a meeting with Helen Grayle. She also secures an early photo of Mrs. Grayle, and throughout the novel she assembles clues and steers Marlowe in fruitful directions. Both he and Randall frequently comment on her exceptional deductive capacities. She also possesses personality traits that are similar to Marlowe's. Professionally she is independent, like him, working as a freelance writer for newspapers; and her general restlessness and curiosity force her to take chances other women of her era would not. Like Marlowe she enjoys driving at night and becomes involved in matters that are really none of her business. When viewing the gruesomely disfigured body of a dead Lindsey Marriott, she is stoical, and Marlowe admires "her nerve" (62).

She is fully capable of trading barbed verbal ripostes with Marlowe, something tough men, but not always women, use to counter his wisecracking. Just as he does, she asks impertinent questions, and she has his ability to look beyond facades to a hidden essence. She frequently knows what he is thinking and recognizes his hard-boiled patter as a defense against vulnerability and full personal disclosure. For all their toughness, each also has a strong sentimental streak. Marlowe continues his investigation of Marriott's death because he feels he failed as a bodyguard, and Riordan removes the reefers from the dead man's body because it would be "kind of mean for the poor man to be found dead with marihuana cigarettes in his pocket" (82).

In yet another important respect Riordan matches Marlowe. In every novel the detective reveals, in spite of his mean profession and tough banter, a cultured sensitivity, especially a love of literature that frequently spills out in the many references or allusions. This novel, in particular, is dotted with all manner of literary references, with Marlowe frequently alluding to Shakespeare's *King Richard III* (for a time a working title of the novel was *The Second Murderer*, a reference to one of the play's minor characters who "had certain dregs of conscience, but still wanted the money" [238]), Hemingway, detective fictions, and nursery rhymes. Riordan is also given to similar literary references, telling a battered Marlowe he looks "like Hamlet's father" (155) and teasing him about his "charming light smile and a phony English accent like Philo Vance" (242).

In all these ways Riordan emerges as Marlowe's equal, not only in the reader's but also in the detective's eyes; and when compared with the ruthless, conniving villainy of Helen Grayle or the shabby manipulativeness of Jessie Florian, Riordan is anything but another of Chandler's stock female characters. In discussing the novelist's characterizations, Dennis Porter contends that "Chandler sets himself the literary task of finding new combinations of words to express models of ugliness, corruption, squalor, evil, and eroticism. The goal is not so much mimesis as astonishment" (65). For the most part Porter is correct; however, Riordan stands as a notable exception to this extraordinary rule.

The question then arises, as Mason implicity asks, why Marlowe continually flees from Riordan's obvious advances. The answer, it seems to me, has far less to do with misogyny or homosexuality than with a view of the world and of women that Marlowe holds. Jerry Speir again helps clarify the situation when writing:

Marlowe's attitude toward women reflects the same conflict between his idealism and his experience which colors all his actions. A part of him longs for the perfect goddess; his experience persistently shatters that dream. When he thinks he has found a person close to his ideal in Anne Riordan, his impulse is to enshrine her. (113-14)

As Chandler repeatedly explained in letters and as the concluding paragraphs of "The Simple Art of Murder" lyrically insist, his version of the detective is a complexly paradoxical figure:

He must be a complete man and a common man and yet an unusual man. He must be, to use a rather weathered phrase, a man of honor—by instinct, by inevitability, without thought of it, and certainly without saying it. He must be the best man in his world and a good enough man for any world. . . . If there were enough like him, the world would be a very safe place to live in, without becoming too dull to be worth living in. ("The Simple Art of Murder," 20-21)

As nearly all critics have noted, Marlowe is a modern knight errant, an exceptionally principled man who must make his way through a dangerous, sordid world.

Like a knight he does indeed idealize women, and in this novel Anne Riordan is placed on a pedestal. But Marlowe is also painfully aware of women like Morgan le Fay and consequently remains on his guard around any woman. To read through Chandler's canon is to find a character, who, at the close of each adventure, becomes increasingly more defeated and world-weary, and each book ends on a note of resignation and defeat despite the relative success of the case.

Marlowe indeed wants to protect Riordan, to shield her first from a police interrogation and later from the gangsters who may discover that she has aided him. He also wants to preserve his hopelessly and certainly unfairly idealized view of her. To accomplish either of these goals, he feels he must remain at a distance, never allowing himself to get too emotionally involved, which has led some critics to view his gallantry as a sign of an imaginative shortcoming on Chandler's part. Dennis Porter speaks for many: "Anne Riordan, an attractive young woman who is also 'nice,' apparently posed a problem for Chandler that he was unable to solve satisfactorily within the terms of the hard-boiled formula and its myths" (187).

Porter, like so many others, once more confuses the author with his creation. The "problem" here (and there is a problem) is not Chandler's but Marlowe's, a problem Chandler has *deliberately* created for his character and of which he is fully aware. In an illuminating letter, Chandler explains, "Marlowe is not a real person. He is a creature of fantasy. He is in a false position because I put him there" ("Letter to Mrs. Robert J. Hogan, March 7, 1947," 232). Marlowe is well aware that his idealism is anachronistic, but he clings to it in spite of the brutality of his world. In the novel's final chapter after learning that Helen Grayle has escaped to Baltimore and committed suicide, he tells Randall that she probably acted out of love and a desire to protect her enfeebled husband. Paraphrasing a line from *Othello*, he explains:

But what she did and the way she did it kept her from coming back here for trial. Think that over. And who would that trial hurt most? Who would be least able to bear it? And win, lose or draw, who would pay the biggest price for the show? An old man who loved not wisely, but too well. (249)

When Randall dismisses this as "just sentimental," Marlowe counters, "'Sure. It sounded like that when I said it. Probably all a mistake anyway'" (249). Yet in the next breath he asks the befuddled Randall if the pink bug he found in the office on his last visit has returned.

Marlowe identifies strongly with this small insect, which has scaled eighteen floors "just to make a friend. Me. *My* luck piece" (184). For Marlowe the bug becomes a symbol of dogged determination and commitment. It faces a seemingly impossible task and succeeds, just as Marlowe faces the brutal impossibilities of his world and retains his determination.

By developing too intimate a relationship with Riordan, Marlowe feels he not only would expose her more directly to the world's harshness but would soon be forced to see her descend from the pedestal. Marlowe is caught between extremes of idealism and reality, and his *failure* is his inability to imagine anything, in this case a woman, as falling somewhere in between these extremes. Marlowe is aware of his self-created predicament, but self-knowledge finally offers no solution to his dilemma.

Such complexities of character and response to the world are markedly absent in the two film versions of the novel, different as they are from one another. In the first of these, *Murder, My Sweet*, Anne Riordan appears as Ann Grayle (altered spelling given her in the film), daughter of Lewin Lockridge Grayle and stepdaughter of Helen. Once again she emerges from the shadows, finding an unconscious Marlowe, but she is startled into running away once he awakens. She appears the next day at his office, dressed in a prim suit and pillbox hat, *pretending* to be a newspaper reporter (the woman has no discernible occupation in the film), prying for information about a lost necklace.

What issues from this meeting and is emphasized in nearly every other encounter with the detective is her complete devotion at all costs to her father, whom she seeks to protect. Lost in the film is the notion of a strong, independent woman with no living relatives; instead, she has been replaced by Daddy's "girl," who tries repeatedly to discourage Marlowe's interest in either Helen or, more important, the case.

When he arrives at her home after his punishing stay at Dr. Sonderborg's, directed accidentally by the address she earlier gave him, Ann is extremely annoyed by the intrusion and insists he leave; throughout the film she oscillates between attraction to and repulsion for the detective. She accuses Marlowe of being unscrupulous, expresses her hatred of Helen, and worries about the repercussions for her father. Nevertheless, he persuades her to visit her father's home, where they learn that Marriott has been living at Grayle's beach home. Once again she is angered by Marlowe's persistence and accuses him of being "vicious" in his disregard for her father.

At the beach house they kiss and embrace; she again berates Marlowe when he suggests, ironically, that she is trying to deflect his attention with affection. Unlike her fictional counterpart, this woman is easily insulted and emotionally brittle, and her sense of ethics is not nearly as developed as Anne Riordan's. For instance, after Mr. Grayle shoots an armed Helen before she can kill Marlowe, Ann tries to prevent Marlowe from calling the police by arguing, "She was evil, all evil. What difference could it possibly make who killed her?"

The film's conclusion, however, offers some of the most marked differences between the two characters. Here Marlowe, eyes blinded by gunpowder, gives a confession and learns that Ann has corroborated his story. As he is led out to a taxi by one detective, he chatters on about the woman's charms and regrets his rough handling of her. Quietly she follows him down in the elevator and enters his cab. As they drive away, he smells her perfume, and they kiss as the camera fades out. In the novel it is Anne who demands, "'I'd like to be kissed, damn you!'" (246), but here a playful Marlowe ironically requests a smooch.

The *Farewell, My Lovely* film of 1975, starring a haggard Robert Mitchum, skillfully evokes the spirit of 1940s Los Angeles with neon-drenched streets and numerous details of dress and setting. Marlowe's interests here are divided between two new and entirely separate characters who have *replaced* Anne Riordan. The first of these is Georgie, a middle-aged newsboy who has a running bet with Marlowe about Joe DiMaggio's famous hitting streak. Georgie is an ex-fighter who shadowboxes and wrestles with Marlowe at the end of each of their encounters.

Georgie allows Marlowe to recuperate at his home after being drugged by Francis Amthor, L.A.'s most famous madman, and in a spirit of male solicitude Georgie provides the sports page and a new pistol. Marlowe later uses Georgie's place to arrange a telephone call between Moose Malloy and Velma. Georgie's final scene comes at the boat docks, where, severely bruised and battered, he informs Marlowe that "I didn't tell 'em anything, Mr. Marlowe."

While the two men obviously enjoy each other's company, there is a distinct pecking order. Marlowe always addresses the boxer by a diminutive form of his first name; however, Georgie never varies from using the curiously formal "*Mr.* Marlowe." Clearly the relationship is marked by a spirit of male camaraderie and a rough version of affection, but absent is the interplay between equals. The two never trade insults, and while Georgie aids Marlowe, he is no match for the detective's professional abilities.

A second character who fills the role of sentimental attraction in the film is the nameless child of Tommy Ray, a once successful bandleader now down on his luck for marrying a black woman. Marlowe is immediately taken with the child's insouciance and his desire to become a baseball player. When Tommy Ray mysteriously vanishes, Marlowe visits the family apartment to check on the boy. Later, when he attempts to convince Nulty (here playing the role of the novel's Randall) to allow him to board Brunette's ship, Marlowe moans, "That kid of Tommy Ray's is gonna haunt me for the rest of my life for letting them kill his old man. He will, you know." Finally, in the film's last scene, Marlowe wanders over to the child's apartment, idly tossing a baseball in the air, intending to give him the $2,000 the detective has earned on the case.

Each of these film depictions alters the character of Anne Riordan in important ways that demonstrate prevailing attitudes about filmmaking and the spirit of their times. With *Murder, My Sweet* the alteration of Riordan into a model of daughterly love and rectitude not only reveals the historical period and its view of young women but also demonstrates the conventions of many female depictions in the film noir genre. Often these women are of unmistakable character and fall into two rigid categories—good and bad (the latter often referred to as "black widows" for their deadly treachery). Ann Grayle is clearly the good one, and Helen Grayle is just as clearly the bad one.[4]

On the other hand, *Farewell, My Lovely*, in eliminating the female character altogether, gives way to the "buddy" motif evident in many films of that era. Movies such as *Butch Cassidy and the Sundance Kid*, *The Sting*, *Deliverance*, and a host of others suggest implicitly and sometimes explicitly that the male bond is primary and in many cases preferable to any profound involvement with a woman as an equal. Indeed, men have dalliances with women, as Mitchum's Marlowe does with Charlotte Rampling's Helen Grayle, but in the end these women are always viewed as disappointing or deceitful and men are left to return to their buddies or go it alone.[5]

It is ironic, then, that Chandler in 1940, in the popular genre of the detective story, created a woman who appears much more like contemporary women than those in either of these films. Chandler felt this was his best novel; and indeed, in this work he explores human relationships and sexual stereotypes with far more intricacy than even his most sympathetic readers may assume. *Farewell, My Lovely*, as much as any of his other books, lives up to the task he set for himself:

To accept a mediocre form and make something like literature out of it is in itself rather an accomplishment. . . . Any man who can write a page of living prose adds something to our life. . . . If you believe in an ideal, you don't own it—it owns you, and you certainly don't want to freeze it at your own level for mercenary reasons. ("Letter to Mrs. Robert J. Hogan, March 7, 1947," 94-95)

NOTES

1. The first cinematic adaptation of the novel was *The Falcon Takes Over* (1942), which I exclude from consideration because only the novel's plot, not its central character, has been preserved.

2. Russell Davies in "Omnes Me Impune Lacessunt" in Miriam Gross, ed., *The World of Raymond Chandler*, makes such an association by arguing that "every page of the Marlowe mysteries bears witness . . . to the struggle between soul-baring and reticence in Raymond Chandler's mind" (32).

3. Chandler was, however, aware of Legman's opinion and wrote in a letter, "Mr. Legman seems to me to belong to that rather numerous class of American neurotics which cannot conceive of a close friendship between a couple of men as other than homosexual."

4. The formula for film noir is discussed in Alain Silver and Elizabeth Ward's *Film Noir: An Encyclopedic Reference to the American Style*, in which they describe *Murder, My Sweet* as an "archetypal" noir production.

5. Peter Wolfe in *Something More Than Night: The Case of Raymond Chandler* views her omission as a result of Marlowe's self-protection from emotional involvement. Al Clark in *Raymond Chandler in Hollywood*, however, quotes screenwriter Zelag Goodman as saying that because of Mitchum's age Riordan was written out of the script (57).

REFERENCES

Chandler, Raymond. *Farewell, My Lovely*. New York: Vintage, 1940.
____. "Letter to Mrs. Robert J. Hogan, March 7, 1947." In *Raymond Chandler Speaking*, edited by Dorothy Gardner and Katerine Sorley Walker. Boston: Houghton Mifflin, 1977.
Clark, Al. *Raymond Chandler in Hollywood*. New York: Proteus, 1982.
____. *The Simple Art of Murder*. New York: Ballantine, 1972.
Davies, Russell. "Omnes Me Impune Lacessunt." In *The World of Raymond Chandler*, edited by Miriam Gross. New York: A & W Publishers, 1977.
Legman, Gershon. *Love and Death: A Study in Censorship*. New York: Hacker Art Books, 1949.
Mason, Michael. "Marlowe, Men and Women." In *The World of Raymond Chandler*, edited by Miriam Gross. New York: A & W Publishers, 1977.
Porter, Dennis. *The Pursuit of Crime*. New Haven, CT: Yale University Press, 1981.
Silver, Alain, and Elizabeth Ward. *Film Noir: An Encyclopedic Reference to the American Style*. Woodstock, NY: Overlook Press, 1979.
Speir, Jerry. *Raymond Chandler*. New York: Frederick Ungar, 1981.
Wolfe, Peter. *Something More Than Night: The Case of Raymond Chandler*. Bowling Green, OH: Popular Press, 1985.

2

Order, Error, and the Novels of Raymond Chandler

Steven Weisenburger

The scene is Chapter 25 of Raymond Chandler's novel *The Big Sleep*. In gruff, cynical tones Harry Jones completes a narrative testimony about Mr. Canino, Eddie Mars, and the mysterious Mona Mars. Philip Marlowe listens, poker-faced, then heads back to his office. "I went upstairs again," Marlowe says, "and sat in my chair thinking about Harry Jones and his story. It seemed a little too pat. It had the austere simplicity of fiction rather than the tangled woof of fact" (BS 158).

Here is a notable formula. Chandler defines fictional narratives as being austerely simple, to the point of being precise, exact, and without need of revision; they are "pat," as Marlowe says. Factual narratives are defined in contrast as being quite the opposite. They are inadequate, radically unfinished, and therefore complex and "tangled." In sum, stories are finished; the world is not. Yet one can rephrase the formula still further to read: Stories are constructed, are products of intention, and can therefore be hermeneutically unpacked or totalized around specific, originary meanings; by contrast the world of "fact" is given, not made, and is therefore ruled by its very unruliness. P. D. James's statement that detective fictions are "small celebrations of order and reason in an increasingly disordered world"—says essentially the same thing.

It is also a very typical formula. Like any detective, one of Marlowe's principal narrative functions is, indeed, to be given, or to request, or even to provoke narrative testimony. Another of his functions is to interpret that evidence. In this capacity Marlowe must reread a character's (putatively factual) testimony as if it were a fictional narrative wherein intention or motive is not only regarded as *the* formal armature but also in a quite contrary sense regarded as engendering— with the duplicitous, guilty witness—the very gaps, contradictions, inadequacies, and errors of narration that successful detection must ferret out and explain.

Harry Jones's account with its "pat" and "austere simplicity of fiction" is therefore doubly significant. By sheer coincidence (as it turns out) he happens to know where Mona Mars is hiding, and he can barter this information to Marlowe. Still, because he's motivated by a grifter's greed Harry misunderstands and thereupon misrepresents, in his "story," the whereabouts of Rusty Regan—who turns out to be the novel's chief enigma.

Yet doesn't this interpretive practice give the lie to that easy formula? Because, if fictions are simple, exact, and complete, if they are "pat," then why would anyone interrogate them for gaps, contradictions, or malfunctions? Or again, if fictional texts stand, in P. D. James's phrase, as "celebrations of order and reason," then how does it make sense also to acknowledge their tendency to disorder and error? We can press this paradox still further. It is a commonplace in the theory of detective fiction that the detective-protagonist can be read as an idealization of the reader. As Todorov, Eco, and numerous others have stated, the detective's interpretive activity models our own. If so, then the detective's ferreting out of gaps, malfunctions, and errors in the narrative testimony of witnesses certainly models (and authorizes) our own interrogation of such signs in the novels themselves.

To my knowledge such an approach to the detective story has yet to be tried. Clearly, doing so could involve the full panoply of Derridean devices whereby (as in *Of Grammatology* or *Limited Inc*) we would approach writing as an unavoidably errant practice, governed by the supplemental and radically uncontrollable energy intervening between act and intention, signifier and signified.[1] Such a thorough deconstructive critique lies well outside the scope of this paper. Yet, the case of Raymond Chandler offers exemplary possibilities, and not only because Marlowe's interpretive work authorizes this approach. Reading his novels against the grain in this way—with an eye for their glitches—can open fresh readings of particular texts, of Chandler's career, and even of the ideological work of that hard-boiled form with which he is so profoundly identified.

The struggle between signs of order and error shapes all the Chandler novels. In one characteristic form, it is figured as an absolute opposition between the detective's reasoned *gambit* and the *gambling* of his villainous antagonists. Carmen Sternwood gambles at Eddie Mars's club in *The Big Sleep*; Helen Grayle is affiliated with casino-operator Laird Brunette in *Farewell, My Lovely*; in *The High Window* Leslie Murdock steals his late father's prize doubloon to cover his gambling debts; Muriel Chess plays roulette in *The Lady in the Lake*; a photograph of the gambler Steelgrave triggers much of the trouble in *The Little Sister*; and Terry Lennox is reviled as "the friend of gamblers" in *The Long Goodbye*. Chapter 48 of this last novel brings one of Marlowe's cop friends, Bernie Ohls, into the pulpit for an uncharacteristically long and vehement antigambling sermon, which connects the vice to dope-pushers, pornographers, and mobsters; it is the symptom of "a disease" threatening the life of modern cities. Marlowe agrees but rationalizes these evils—in a revealing comment—as "the price we pay *for organization*" (LG 290 [emphasis added]). He thus reads gambling and all its attendant mass-cultural evils as *natural* disorders of orderly systems, as if to claim there is a Murphy's Law for rationalized, modern society, according to which axiom the irrationality of drugs and gambling are predictable, symptomatic results of an overdetermined industrial order.

There is no other moment like this in the Chandler canon, in which gamblers and their gunsels, like Canino in *The Big Sleep* or *The Little Sister*'s Weepy Moyer, are otherwise always reviled—and finally gunned down. This later-day admission accepts gambling—or coincidence and chance in the most general sense—as "natural" or at least understandable (as well as marginal) symptoms of any orderly or logically determined system—perhaps of narrative systems as well.

In Chandler's narrative system the counterpart of gambling is Marlowe's chess games, which aren't really "games" at all. Rather, his contests reenact famous matches—"four or five movers" or the "French defense against Steinitz" (LG 10). Within such already-scripted potentials Marlowe achieves outcomes worked out according to traditional, orderly, and logically determined contingencies. In *The High Window* Marlowe comments that there is "a whole literature about chess" from which he draws (HW 86); and the conservative *plotted* conditions for gaming are both analogous to detective work and fraught with ideological power. In Chapter 26 of *The Lady in the Lake* Marlowe's thoughts turn away in revulsion from the mass-cultural chaos of Bay City and toward orderly gaming: "Time to go home," he thinks, "and get your slippers and play over a game of chess" (LL 143). The phrase "play over" means just that: To replay what is foreknown. This is why Marlowe plays chess when "thinking things out" on a case, when he is reasoning through the complex (but often self-consciously novelistic or cinematic) plots of suspects and trying "to fit the things [he] knows into a pattern," as he says in *The Little Sister* (LS 146). In *The Long Goodbye* this pattern-seeking ability underwrites Marlowe's final judgment on Terry Lennox: Explaining why he bolted from the scene of his wife's murder, Terry comments, "A man can't figure every angle that quick" (LG 309). A chess-player's admission of defeat, this remark leads directly into Marlowe's condemnation of the man for his lack of "ethics or scruples." As a rebuke of a novelist's failure to separate errancy from intentionality, it has further significance.

Order and error are always battling for ascendancy in Chandler's fictions, although in the most general terms that *agon* is basic to detective stories. Thus, conventional interpretations of specific texts will highlight narrative structures that build toward moments of provisional and then final *denouement*, a totalizing mininarrative when, as Marlowe says in prefacing one such paragraph in *The Big Sleep*'s last chapter, "It all ties together—everything" (BS 209). In these moments "everything" is revealed as plotted, not only in the sense that the detective recognizes events as being paradoxically ordered by characters' transgressive, errant desires but also in the sense that his superior ratiocinative, ordering faculty can contain their plots within his own narration. Yet reading the stories in this way—reading them *with* the grain, and with the detective as an idealized form of readerly desire—requires a remarkable blindness to their equally significant gaps, indeterminacies, contradictions and errors.

Even Chandler's most apparently unified, closed-end narratives reveal deep fissures and remarkable glitches, and reckoning with such moments can shed fresh light on the most basic conventions of the genre. One of the commonest critical presuppositions about the form, for example, is that the detective's work must culminate in naming and arresting the representative of some lawless desire. But Chandler's texts generally turn on representations of desire as not only a "dangerous supplement," but something utterly redundant as well: Desire keeps pressing and reinsinuating its demands, for instance, in the form of blackmail. Here is Marlowe on the subject in *The Little Sister*: "I always wonder why people pay blackmailers. They can't buy a anything. Yet, they do pay them, sometimes over and over and over again. And in the end they're just where they started" (LS 115). This is because neither the blackmail-victim nor the detective can get back to origins. In *The Big Sleep*, *The High Window*, and *The Little Sister*, images from a photographic negative can be endlessly reduplicated in the form of "a positive made from the negative and another negative made from the positive," as Marlowe points out (LS 115). Such observations make intriguing claims about the functioning of desire in the form of doubles and simulacra. The notable aspect, though, is Marlowe's admitted inability to recoup, much less erase, the image of an "original" lapse. That inability might well be taken as a *mise en abyme* for the genre itself. Yet, there are numerous other subplots that are similarly problematic: The obsessive sexual lapses of characters like Carmen Sternwood (in *The Big Sleep*) or Dolores Gonzales (*The Little Sister*) or the serialized identity-switches of characters like Helen Grayle (in *Farewell, My Lovely*), Mildred Chess (*The Lady in the Lake*), and Terry Lennox (*The Long Goodbye*). Indeed, though critics don't deal with the problem, it is clear that Marlowe never learns the original identity of Paul Marston-Terry Lennox-Senor Maioranos, just as he doesn't in the case of the wonderfully named Mildred Chess. In such instances the detective's work falls far short of the ideal. Instead of arresting the originators of a lawless desire, it is more a business of fingering some (admittedly guilty) scapegoat, the reader having already glimpsed reciprocal, violent desire as a quite general, ongoing crisis well beyond the efforts of any heroic knight's gambit.

In other ways, too, the inexplicable, or the coincidental, or the narratological lapse or gap always threatens to undo the form. *The Big Sleep*, in many ways Chandler's tightest and best-edited work of hard-boiled detection, provides a telling case in point. Critical comment sometimes pauses over relatively minor cruxes in detail, such as the question about who killed Owen Taylor that prompted a telegraph from film producer Howard Hawks: Chandler reportedly rechecked his text and replied, "I don't know." Much more problematic, yet scarcely ever analyzed, is the question of how Marlowe *knows* it was Carmen who killed Rusty Regan and dropped his corpse into an oil sump on the Sternwood property. One reader, usually an acute chronicler of such details in plotting, simply writes that "Marlowe has outsmarted her. Although she believes she has lured him to a spot where she can kill him safely, he has tricked her *into reenacting the Regan murder*" (Wolfe 122, my emphasis).[2] But such statements entail reading over a sizable narrative chasm, for Chandler's text not only shoves Marlowe's recognition of Carmen's guilt entirely offstage, which would still be conventional enough, it also oversteps any retrospective summary of *how* he knew, *when* Carmen tipped her hand, or, for that matter, *what* other clues might be interpreted as residuals of Carmen's original crime. Readers thus have no means of saying how Marlowe's dangerous stratagem took shape.

When and on the strength of what evidence has Marlowe "outsmarted" Carmen? The question is unanswerable because it hovers over an absolute gap in the narrative. No logic of causality or sequentiality, of deduction or even inferences can explain the actions of Chapters 31 and 32. The only feasible explanation is from the rhetoric of doubles and simulacra: Carmen's attempted murder "plays over" an earlier plot, as a "reenacting" of Rusty's murder. This remains our only source for *feelings* of closure and unity, beyond the misogynist's satisfaction of getting back to a hissing, catlike woman, aptly named Carmen, fingered as the source of every mortal corruption in this narrative world. With *The Big Sleep*, then, any attempt to make the novel jibe with the supposedly deductive, Aristotelian orderings of the detective genre, as well as the ethically simple world of vigilantism, seems rather too "pat." Ideologically, such a narrative has more to do with uncovering threats of a vamping, murderous mass culture, a consumer society repeatedly indexed by Carmen's "cloying perfume," the "flash" of her clothes and her gambling, as well as by her extraordinary feline "hissing noise" and "small corrupt body." Rushing to uncover this horror, Chandler disregards other narratological lapses.

Like this first novel, Chandler's subsequent fictions often turn on coincidences too bizarre for readers to naturalize them under the familiar conventions of the detective story. *The Lady in the Lake*, for example, hinges on the impossible idea that two women who do not know each other, Muriel Chess and Crystal Kingsley, not only look but also talk enough alike to be identical twins and that they moreover cross paths at precisely the right moment for Chess to murder Kingsley, dump the body in Little Fawn Lake, and commence successfully to impersonate the woman even among Kingsley's acquaintances. *The Long Goodbye* asks readers to believe that a speedboat operated by someone completely outside Eileen Wade's murder plot just happens to backfire at the exact moment needed for her to camouflage the report of the pistol she uses to murder her husband Roger and to do it in a way that will be read as suicide. Once again, this list could go on, for there are moments in all Chandler's later fictions when chance and coincidence overthrow any conventions of causality, sequence, or order in the detective formula. Some moments call attention, instead, to an obsessive fantasizing played out with doubles and eerie simulations.

Chandler would become increasingly self-conscious about these disruptions, but in the early novels they never bother him. To his narrator, coincidences are simply accidents of fortune awaiting his retrospective and final detection of causes. "Proof," Marlowe remarks in *Farewell, My Lovely* (1940), will always emerge from "an overwhelming balance of probabilities" evaluated after the fact and despite how improbable they at first may have seemed (FL 167). Initially, then, such categories as fiction/fact or order/disorder remain stabilized for Chandler, even during his writing of novels like Sleep or *Farewell*, plotted as they are around notable gaps and incredible coincidences.

By his third novel, *The High Window* (1942), there are multiplying signs of instability. The unbelievable plot coincidences are more frequent and more obvious, because more wildly improbable and also because Chandler calls attention to them. On tossed-away matches Marlowe finds an inscribed name miraculously unburned. Later, a witness turns over to him a bill of sale that just happened to flutter from a key suspect's pocket, a bill the witness just happened to save although it is virtually meaningless to him, but that just happens to put Marlowe on the scent of a counterfeiting scam that's secondary to but (incredibly) bound up with the primary plot. Yet the novel's main plot also involves the inconceivable chance of a total stranger's getting a snapshot of this novel's villainess, Mrs. Elizabeth Bright Murdock, pushing her late husband from the window of a high-rise office building. Equally as wild are the random circumstances of Marlowe's finding a print of this photo in the ransacked room of the murdered blackmailer, Vannier. When asked to explain, Marlowe acknowledges the infinitesimally small probabilities, commenting that his finding the image was "a fluke of the same sort that was involved in the taking of the picture; which is a fair sort of justice" (HW 201). Thus, we are still offered the metaphor of probabilities held in balance; it is a "poetic justice" in the literal sense, in having more to do with the doubling of rhetorical figures than any concern for social reality. Also, Marlowe's remark points up the fiction's self-consciousness about such plottings, which seems still greater when read in context with other moments of metafictional commentary in *Window*. In a scene at the "Idle Valley Club," a sort of upper-class speakeasy, Marlowe mocks the place as running "so true to type," right down to the clichéd torch singer and her "hard-boiled vocabulary." Elsewhere, he derisively compares himself to fictional detective Philo Vance, and other scenes take on a "B-picture" quality to him. In these moments Chandler's fiction begins recognizing the unruly power of its own narrative practices, or for that matter of any *writing*. The too-simple boundaries of "fiction" and "fact" begin to blur, and his novels will be more cynically self-conscious about such matters from here on. Increasingly, too, Marlowe complains of having lapsed into a late-modern, media-induced, or "B-picture" society, an ontologically indecipherable world in which all signifiers, including his own, might be construed as figures in a fictive plot strewn with "cute meets" and trick denouements.

In the early Chandlers, reality often seems hazy. *The Big Sleep*'s penultimate struggle occurs at "Realito"—ironically named, given the fogs and Marlowe's dazed sense of the place. *Farewell* also has its too-conventional fogs "that make everything seem so unreal"; and *Window*, borrowing a motif from *Sleep*, begins from a green-room of rioting plant-life and "winy" smells that seem "unreal" (HW 9). But only in Chandler's middle fictions does that boundary between reality and simulacra decisively blur. *The Lady in the Lake* (1943) involves the wildest set of coincidences in all of Chandler's work: Not only the Muriel Chess/Crystal Kingsley look-alikes, but numerous bits of evidence too cutely found and the ridiculous circumstances (in retrospect) that are needed for police sergeant Degarmo, one of Muriel's ex-husbands, *not* to solve the mystery long before the novel's rather anticlimactic end. Strewn everywhere through this tangle of impossible "flukes" are Marlowe's acknowledgments of their great improbability, asides best read as metacomments on the stresses Chandler recognizes in the form. Those gestures often prompt critics to read the novel as a parody. It isn't, and not only because there is no shred of evidence, textual or biographical, to suggest Chandler intended to write it as one. The novel only seems parodic when its overdetermined and self-conscious narrative is read from a campy, late-modernish standpoint.

The Lady in the Lake is the last Chandler novel to have Marlowe worrying, metafictionally, over the coincidences all around him. In the long, six-year dry spell between *Lady* and the beginning of his final phase, Chandler's focus widens. *Writing* becomes Marlowe's most common metaphor, and with good reason. Chandler had tried to push them off his desk, but signs of chance and coincidence kept insinuating themselves into the texts. Now Chandler's narratives show him realizing how the writing, all along, has been driven by simulations and doublings, by errant coincidences and unanticipated "flukes" as much as by controlled intention and deductive orders. Not only a knight's gambit, his fictions are built on recognizable writerly gambles. And, perhaps the most troubling paradox to him, he realizes that his is precisely the kind of lucrative, mass-market writing that, he has been exchanging for financial independence, while at the same time, in the novels themselves he has written increasingly vociferous monologues against the same mass culture he derogates as a vile (and usually feminine) body.

There were already signs of this last phase in *Lady*. That novel includes numerous images and metaphors of writing, such as Muriel Chess's apparent suicide note, Crystal Kingsley's letters, and other notes that track readers through key clues. Marlowe keeps one of them, reeking of perfume, in his coat pocket and hauls it out several times, as if weirdly attracted to its author. Moreover, the novel's plot hinges on the idea of a scripted reality, in the Kingsley cabin's too-well-ordered domestic environment that will bring the undoing of Muriel Chess. Crystal was an untidy person, but when Marlowe examines them the rooms are too neat, and this detail triggers Marlowe's solution of the crime. At novel's end he comments that it was Muriel's need to "edit the job," to "make sure it was all in order," that unraveled her nearly perfect crime (LL 211). Thus her most often used name attains a special significance: As Mrs. *Chess*, her error was in seeking and finally overdoing the ideal of scriptable, deductive order. Muriel's error was that of *the writer*, as Marlowe/Chandler had realized it in writing the earlier novels.

Published six years after *Lady*, *The Little Sister* (1949) intensifies all of these signs and symptoms. It therefore might be read as the quintessential Chandler story, in contrast to the many critics who read it as an eccentrically angry and unsuccessful book.[3] On my reading, *The Little Sister* simply reveals Chandler's characteristic (and even obsessive) desires for order in a corrupted modern world, desires triggered by perceived threats of a contemporary, media-induced society where everything seems scripted, therefore erring. Orrin Quest, innocent Kansan turned vicious killer in "the department store state" of California, learns the fine art of ice-pick murders from reading newspaper stories. Everyone is in, or wants to be in, pictures; and they all, Marlowe included, experience life as cinematic text. "This was happening somewhere else in a cheesy program picture," thinks Marlowe, observing (in slow motion) a man aim a gun at him (LS 85). Mavis Weld, a.k.a. Leila Quest, the missing big sister, "can't think of any lines" when Marlowe interrogates her (LS 196). Later, when he begins adding up the evidence, she counters: "I guess I just don't like the script. . . . It just isn't me" (LS 203). Even minor characters adopt mass-cultural roles, like police detectives Beifus and French, who play out a kind of raunchy, homo-sexually charged Abbott and Costello routine. By novel's close, then, Marlowe can only sum up the metaphor that has run throughout: "The play was over. I was sitting in the empty theater" (237). Then he drives the little sister, Orfamay Quest, back to Kansas, away from this world of seamy simulacra, of scripted signifiers that dream wearily of origins. He returns her to a presumably "authentic" America in the Midwest, where Chandler himself was born.

Of all Chandler's novels, *Sister* also functions the most obsessively by a logic of doublings. There are numerous double identities: Mavis Weld changed her name from Leila Quest; the gangster Steelgrave was previously a Cleveland icepick murderer named Weepy Moyer; one of Orrin's victims, Dr. G. W. Hambleton, was previously known as George W. Hicks, and before that as "Mileaway Marston . . . a runner for Ace Devore" (LS 61). And there are double murders: Lester Clausen and Hambleton, ice-picked by Orrin Quest. And double trouble, in the form of double crosses and blackmail plots, or twin bone-handled revolvers, or the relentless enticements of Mavis Weld and Dolores Gonzales, who respectively embody the lighter and darker sides of Chandler's evil vamp. Mavis has simply gotten into trouble by indirection, by the accidents of her climb toward stardom. But of all Chandler's vamps, "the Gonzales" wants it all: She is easily the most lascivious ("Reeking with sex. Utterly beyond the moral laws of this or any world I could imagine," thinks Marlowe [LS 248]), but also the most closely tied to contemporary mass culture. Like *The Big Sleep*'s Carmen Sternwood—or, for that matter, like any of

Chandler's villainous vamps—Dolores Gonzales "hisses" and "spits" when cornered. Far more than Carmen Sternwood, in her films Dolores Gonzales is, Marlowe realizes, the simulacrum of desire for all those middle-class people he finds abjectly disgusting: All the "tired men" who live out in the suburbs amid "the whining of their spoiled children and the gabble of their spoiled wives" (LS 79). There are passages like this scattered throughout the book.

Jerry Speir characterizes *The Little Sister* as Chandler's most misanthropic writing (57-58). To be more concise, the novel takes as the target of its vilification not man in general but mass man and the society of commodified desires, ecstatic simulations, contemporary media, and especially the "scripted" experiences they all (in Chandler's view) induce. As foretold by each of his earlier novels, this late-modern condition now stands as *the* primary villain of the piece, and there is simply nothing conclusive for his detective to do except to clean up people's messes (Mavis Weld's and Dolores Gonzales's, for example) and return shell-shocked psyches (Orfamay Quest's) back to Kansas from Oz. It makes no sense, then, to complain with Speir and other critics that this narrative is flawed because Chandler has failed to work backward through causes and pin guilt on a single criminal: There *is* no sharply individuated guilt; there are only movies, and at novel's end the characters just resume making them.

With its redoubled doublings, *The Little Sister* recalls each of Chandler's earlier detective stories in seeking to restore order by naming the originator of a serial criminality, but in accomplishing that goal in only the most provisional and contingent terms. Again and again, Chandler's fictions had settled for targeting the figure of a woman—like Carmen Sternwood, Velma Valento, Muriel Chess, or Eileen Wade—to stand in for the mass culture and "media-scape" that will give Chandler, in *The Long Goodbye* (1953), something more to rage against: television. This media-induced civilization, a glimpse of that postmodern "hyper-reality" defined recently by Jean Baudrillard and Umberto Eco, comprises the main social reality to which Chandler's later novels make their angriest references. Indeed, so fully are Chandler's fictions determined to disparage these emergent conditions that he forgets various narratological details. He will neglect, for example, what Marlowe has or has not been told. He will curiously invert the character traits assigned to the proper names, Beifus and French, who inexplicably switch roles at novel's end.[4] Such errors and instabilities might well be taken as an inverse gauge of the stability and inerrancy Chandler's ideological police work seeks to achieve in late-modern America.

The Long Goodbye brings these tendencies to a remarkable climax. Chandler has Marlowe once more raging against contemporary mass culture and its "scripted" realities. He chafes at being made to play unwittingly his role in Terry Lennox's getaway plot and faked suicide, and he suspects Eileen Wade of having "written a script" for his visit to Dr. Verringer's clinic (LG 123). From the novel's "society page dog vomit" and television wrestlers (LG 12), to the "billion-dollar industry" of sex and "sex-conscious advertising" strategies (LG 17), Marlowe now takes aim at a far wider range of targets than fourteen years earlier in *The Big Sleep*, where gambling was the chief culprit. Notably, though, for the first time Marlowe also displays a sense of the historical processes behind these conditions. Responding to Harlan Potter, who uses wealth to shield himself from a popular culture he also vilifies, Marlowe scoffs at the old man's desire to uphold "the way . . . people lived fifty years ago before the age of mass production" (LG 192). Yet even despite this awareness Marlowe will rage on, with old police friend Bernie Ohls and others, against the perceived excesses of mass culture. In retrospect this hypocrisy seems crucially typical of American modernist ideology: Welcoming the democratic benefits of industrial modernization from one side of the mouth, while from the other deploring in aesthetic texts the perceived loss of authenticity and "real" values in an age of mechanical reproduction.

In *Goodbye*, these contradictions are embodied in the character of novelist Roger Wade. A mass-market success, Wade mirrors Chandler in disavowing his "twelve best-sellers" and aspiring to greater "artistic" achievements. Wade derogates himself to Marlowe as "a literary prostitute or pimp" (LG 142). Like Chandler, Wade is a writer guilty about having double-crossed his own loftier ambitions. In a notable digression that otherwise takes readers nowhere, Marlowe spends an evening over a magazine tale "about a guy that had two lives and two psychiatrists, one was human and one was some kind of insect in a hive" (LG 180). Of course, the "guy" is Wade, whose sensibilities *are* split in two and who does (in effect) have two psychiatrists—Marlowe, who coolly cares for Wade, and Dr. Verringer, later depicted in Wade's own stream-of-consciousness writings as a vile, homosexual queen bee. The point is that for Chandler, the popular writer can exist only as a divided personality and in awful subservience to the demands of the hive, which is American mass civilization.

The Long Goodbye also recalls its predecessors in camouflaging its many narrative "flukes" and doublings. However, this plot depends on a logic of doubles perhaps more than any other Chandler text, and for the first time Marlowe insinuates himself among these simulations. An extraordinarily close male sympathy develops for the first time in Chandler, initially between Marlowe and Terry Lennox, then with Roger Wade ("You're like me," Wade tells him [LG 122]); and Eileen Wade fantasizes that her lost love, Paul Marston, has returned after ten years in the person of Marlowe (coincidentally they have the same initials). Another avatar of Chandler's horrible "queen bee," Eileen tries to seduce Marston/Marlowe, and he nearly succumbs. Then it turns out that Terry Lennox *is* "Marston," though who he may have been prior to that remains undetected. Moreover, it turns out—incredibly—that Terry coincidentally crossed paths with Eileen in Hollywood, rekindling her memories and bringing on the double murder of Lennox's wife, Terry thinking that he's bludgeoned Sylvia to death when in fact Eileen had gotten there first. In other ways, too, the novel plays out familiar Chandler motifs, from antigambling sermonettes to a feline Mrs. Wade who hisses and spits when sexually aroused, like Carmen Sternwood or Mrs. Grayle. To the critics, though, the new wrinkle in this text is Marlowe's increased sexuality; but even this occurs *as a result of* his immersion in the simulations around him in "Bay City." He does wind up in bed with Eileen Wade, though only until her animality leaves him limp and sends him home to the old reliable chessboard. Then, in the closing chapters, Marlowe will for the first time consummate an attraction (to Linda Loring), a moment widely read as a sign that Marlowe's high ideals have finally been "realistically" tempered by the "nastiness" around him.

This may be, but it leaves aside the far more significant connection between sex and writing. *Goodbye* does give Marlowe his sexual debut. However, in this novel Chandler for the first time literalizes his prior metaphors of a scriptable reality by bringing onstage a writer and his texts. Marlowe knows Roger Wade's best-selling "historical romances" and describes them as "tripe," a dismissal echoed by Wade's wife and his literary agent. Wade also disparages his twelve books as inauthentic, mere commodities. As he composes while drunk, Marlowe is amazed to discover the orderly neatness of his typed manuscripts, a further sign of the contrariety of the writing process, as Chandler sees it. To Wade, who reflects upon it in pages of drunken ramblings offered in Chapter 28, writing is also an abjectly sexual process, uncontrollable and degraded: "I could vomit just thinking about the lousy racket," he begins (LG 165), in a phrase that recalls Marlowe's vilification of the "society page dog vomit" he reads. Writing makes Wade "smell foul" to himself. He goes to his writing desk because the only other choice is bed, which he rules out because sleep promises to regurgitate the same vague nightmare of animalistic sex that he recalls as bringing him "an orgasm." By contrast, his writing is frankly masturbatory because it enacts, as Wade puts it, "a beautiful love for myself—and the sweet part of it—no rivals" (LG 166).

All of this is the more remarkable when readers keep in mind that Wade's stream-of-consciousness ramblings are as genuine as writing ever gets in Chandler's world. "I'm not asking any money for it," Wade remarks to himself in justifying a shoddy sentence (LG 166). Indeed, as notebook entries his stream-of-consciousness sentences are intended to stand entirely outside the flux of commodified, popular works that Wade and Marlowe everywhere disparage. Wade's pages are intensely private and readers must ungraciously eavesdrop on them, for Wade has already had Marlowe promise to "tear up" his "crazy stuff." The idea is that everything in the situation of their writing, as well as in their extempore rhetoric underscores what modernist writing values as "authentic": These are the transcribed thoughts, recollected in tranquility, of isolated, monadic consciousness. Even so, disturbances quickly enter the field. Wade mocks his writing for a "Goddam silly simile," and belittles his writerly desire to make "Everything . . . be like something else" (LG 165). He can't rid his page of the popular discourses swarming around him. He therefore begins to understand *any* writing, popular or private, as an unavoidably erring practice.

By extension, Chandler's own writings stand convicted here as a "silly" simulation. Like Wade's masturbatory fantasy of animalistic females, writing is figured in this chapter as a truly dangerous supplement, bound up not only with destructive sexual practices but also with deadly bouts of drunkenness. Writing can never lose itself in an empyrean free from the error-strewn and "nasty" mundanities of mass culture. Instead, the written text is too disorderly, too unpredictable, therefore a defiled body. Like Chandler's mass cultural vamps, writing embodies vertiginous desires and nearly brings on fits of vomiting. Writing is thus the final metaphor of an uncontrollable, feminine, mass cultural Other that Chandler had always been trying to police. But writing was also his only means of scripting the arrest of that Other. How to resolve such a paradox? Except for "The Pencil" and three epigonous chapters of his "Poodle Springs" novel, Chandler stops writing for his remaining seven years.

The increasing self-reflexivity of Chandler's fictions, culmiminating in *The Long Goodbye*, suggests that he knew what was at stake. Raymond Chandler was writing checks against an account of orderly, deterministic aesthetic conventions for detective fiction that his own narrative practices (or *any* writing) would drive into bankruptcy. Still, he had found ways to sustain that conflict creatively by overcoding it in his narrative structures and in Marlowe's cynical metacomments. Put another way, he had found a hero who could still articulate a discourse of apparently stable order and virtue, at the same time as the hero's metadiscourse put over a profound doubt about the artificiality and even the erring contrivances of that order and stability. Thus his last novel concludes, significantly, in "*imitation* marble corridors," with the proclamation of Terry Lennox (or whatever his name is, for the text never does get back to *that* origin): "An act is all there is. There isn't anything else" (LG 311). Look for flaws in the painted backdrop, this man without a name might as well have said.

In cinematic narration some of the narrative malfunctions I have described in this chapter would be classified as "continuity errors": Delightful signs of imperfection, for example, when the scriptwriters or set-dressers neglect a detail necessary to the apparent unity and realism of the director's completed simulacrum. Even the best directors miss such errant signs, and one may well ask: Why? What were they concentrating on instead? Chandler's erring stories are reminders that the detective novel or, for that matter, any text tends to be undone by the very demands for totalizing order and closure that often drive its writing or reading. But such flaws and fissures are also interpretive openings. As I've suggested here, they are lenses on conflicts that are biographical, formal, and eventually ideological. They can thus be crucial reminders. When we ask a text to maintain order amid some perceived chaos exterior to it, shouldn't we also ask: Whose order? On what terms? How, and for whom, does that suppression work?

NOTES

For helpful advice while writing and revising this chapter, I am grateful to my colleague John Cawelti and to the graduate students in my Narrative Theory Seminar of spring 1993.

1. On narrative errors and their interpretation see my "Errant Narrative and *The Color Purple*." Narrative errors have been documented in a great range of fictions, as I suggest in those pages. Yet the interpretive potentials of errors have never been given a disciplined analysis, much less a theoretical framework. There are reasons for correcting that neglect, however. Not only does narratology provide frameworks for defining and categorizing the types of narrative mistakes critics have noted, but deconstructive reading sometimes works by foregrounding such errant and arbitrary textual signs as typos and the like. In their recent study of Pynchon, Alec McHoul and David Wills— working from Derrida's *Of Grammatology* and *Limited Inc*—argue that "The question of error then is indistinguishable from the question of how writing has meaning" (122). In their approach, foregrounding error means backgrounding and thus providing a more distanced and differential view of structures for naturalizing meaning. For a broader treatment of error in deconstructive thought see also Mark C. Taylor's 1984 book, *Erring*. Dialogics also poses important problems for the study of narrative error. In their analysis of Bakhtin's thought, for example, Morson and Emerson have commented on key passages in his writing that affiliate desires for inerrancy with the ideal of a unified, systematic monologism; dialogism, by contrast, "recognizes" (in Bakhtin's words) "only one principle of cognitive individualization: Error" (Morson and Emerson 236).

2. Peter Wolfe tries to reason his way over the gap. From a 1954 letter treating such problems, he quotes Chandler: "There is always a point at which the hero stops taking the reader into his confidence. There is the solution which turns on a recondite piece of knowledge . . . [and] there is the solution which depends on something not disclosed to the reader until almost the end" (the full text of this letter appears in Pepper 29). Wolfe takes this as justifying a solution that is worked out "offstage." But in fact Wolfe has only named the real problems with chapters 31 and 32 of *Sleep*: What was the "recondite piece of knowledge" that fingered Carmen? And why wasn't this solution "disclosed" to us anywhere, much less at "almost the end"? Wolfe never takes up such problems, and that's still more notable because he persists (like most critics) in reading Chandler under the rubrics of realist narrative. For comparable readings see Beekman, Grella, Guetti, Jameson, and Rabinowitz.

3. See for example Wolfe, who reads the novel as "as a further installment in Chandler's poison-pen letter to women" (180), then goes on to defend that misogyny by staying within the story-world and arguing that Chandler's men should have known better. Or see Speir, who reads it as Chandler's most misanthropic book (57-58).

4. Wolfe notes the reversal in the character traits of Beifus and French. In Chapter 11, French is "decent, astute, and professional," while Beifus "peppers his speech with homosexual provocations and sadistic threats"; but in Chapters 29 and 31, when they reappear, these traits are reversed. There were other errors, too: in Chapter 15 Marlowe confronts Orfamay Quest about her sister Leila (Mavis Weld), and Orfamay remarks that she cannot recall telling Marlowe anything about her big sister. She's right, but Marlowe (and Chandler) press on despite the lapse.

REFERENCES

Parenthetical citations to the novels of Raymond Chandler are abbreviated as follows:
   The Big Sleep, BS; *Farewell, My Lovely*, FL; *The High Window*, HW; *The Long   Goodbye*, LG; *The Lady in the Lake*, LL; *The Little Sister*, LS.
Beekman, E. M. "Raymond Chandler and an American Genre." *Massachusetts Review*
   14 (1973): 149-73.
Chandler, Raymond. *The Big Sleep*. 1939. Reprint. New York: Vintage, 1976.
____. *Farewell, My Lovely*. 1940. Reprint. New York: Vintage, 1988.
____. *The High Window*. 1942. Reprint. New York: Vintage, 1976.
____. *The Lady in the Lake*. 1943. Reprint. New York: Vintage, 1976.
____. *The Little Sister*. 1949. Reprint. New York: Vintage, 1988.
____. *The Long Goodbye*. 1953. Reprint. New York: Ballantine, 1971.
Derrida, Jacques. *Of Grammatology*. Trans. Gayatri Chakravorty Spivak. 1st American
   ed. Baltimore: Johns Hopkins University Press, 1979.
____. *Limited Inc*. Evanston, IL: Northwestern University Press, 1988.
Eco, Umberto. "Narrative Structures in Fleming." In *The Role of the Reader*, 144-74.
   Bloomington: Indiana University Press, 1979.
Grella, George. "Murder and the Mean Streets: The Hard-Boiled Detective Novel."
   Contempora 1, no. 1 (1970): 6-15.
Guetti, James. "Aggressive Reading: Detective Fiction and Realistic Narrative." *Raritan*
   2 (1982): 133-54.
Jameson, Frederic. "On Raymond Chandler." *Southern Review* 6 (1970): 624-50.
McHoul, Alec, and David Wills. *Writing Pynchon: Strategies in Fictional Analysis*.
   Urbana: University of Illinois Press, 1990.
Morson, Gary Saul, and Caryl Emerson. *Mikhail Bakhtin: Creation of a Prosaics*. Stan-
   ford, CA: Stanford University Press, 1990.
Pepper, James, ed. *Letters: Raymond Chandler and James M. Fox*. Santa Barbara, CA:
   Neville, 1978.
Rabinowitz, Peter. "'Rats Behind the Wainscotting': Politics, Convention, and Chandler's
   The Big Sleep." *Texas Studies in Literature and Language* 22 (1980): 224-45.
Speir, Jerry. *Raymond Chandler*. New York: Ungar, 1981.
Taylor, Mark C. *Erring*. Chicago: University of Chicago Press, 1984.
Todorov, Tzvetan. "The Typology of Detective Fiction." In *The Poetics of Prose*,
   translated by Richard Howard, 42-52. Ithaca, NY: Cornell University Press, 1977.
Weisenburger, Steven. "Errant Narrative and *The Color Purple*." *Journal of Narrative
   Technique* 19, no. 3 (1989): 257-76.
Wolfe, Peter. *Something More Than Night: The Case of Raymond Chandler*. Bowling
   Green, OH: Bowling Green University Press, 1985.

3

Raymond Chandler's Pencil

James O. Tate

In a remarkable act of homage, twenty-three mystery writers contributed short stories to a volume assembled by Byron Preiss in 1988 as a "Centennial Celebration" of Raymond Chandler. In 1990 that book, *Raymond Chandler's Philip Marlowe*, reappeared as a trade paperback from Perigee Books, replete with stylish illustrations and an introduction by Frank MacShane, Chandler's biographer.

The nostalgic imitations and affectionate pastiches are fun to read. Again and again, the various authors declare in separate notes how much they owe to Chandler as a model and an inspiration. But the best part of the book is the twenty-fourth story by Raymond Chandler himself. His final story, "The Pencil," is the last one in Preiss's anthology, as though it were Chandler's imitation of himself.

And so it is. "The Pencil" was the first short story Chandler wrote in the twenty years since he'd concluded his apprenticeship in pulp magazines such as *Black Mask* and *Dime Detective* and begun his Philip Marlowe novels with *The Big Sleep* in 1939. "The Pencil" appeared posthumously as "Marlowe Takes on the Syndicate" in the *London Daily Mail*, April 6-10, 1959, and as "Wrong Pigeon" in *Manhunt*, February 1961. Reprinted as "The Pencil," the story has not been easy to find since appearing in *The Midnight Raymond Chandler* (1971) and is itself sufficient reason for acquiring *Raymond Chandler's Philip Marlowe*.

Chandler returned to the short story form at the end of his life, I suspect, because he did not have the stuff for another novel. He felt obliged to produce pages of Chandleresque discourse, though he was dying, and he did so. Today, I think we can see that a weak work like "The Pencil," displaying so much of his style and expressing, too, so much of Chandler's self-awareness, is as representative of his work as his stronger efforts. Beneath the surface, this melodramatic story is about the *melos* of its play with language and the drama of its own composition rather than the ostensible "mystery" that is ritually "solved."

"The Pencil" opens with Ikky Rossen's appeal for protection from the Mob or "Outfit" that he has run out on. Marlowe recruits the aid of Anne Riordan (last seen in *Farewell, My Lovely*, 1940) who absurdly spots two arriving hit men at the L.A. airport. Marlowe outmuscles a mug sent to intimidate him and to get Ikky out of town. He then receives a pencil by special delivery to indicate that, like Ikky, he too has been "pencilled" by the Mob. Marlowe soon witnesses the rubout of a man who looks like Ikky in front of Ikky's apartment house. In response to a wire and more interfering intimidation, Marlowe heads for Flagstaff to find Ikky. There he accuses him of a setup: Ikky was not Ikky, the other guy was, and Marlowe was pulled in to even an old score. Soon Marlowe is back in L.A. for champagne at Romanoff's with Anne Riordan, case closed.

Reading "The Pencil," I can see why William H. Marling wrote of it in 1986, "It is an awful pastiche of dated tough-guy dialogue, modern revelations about the Cosa Nostra, and predictable plotting. Chandler fans should avoid it" (71). But Marling assumes that Chandler's other works were *not* awful pastiches of dated tough-guy dialogue. Chandler fans should not avoid "The Pencil"—they should read it to know Chandler. Early and late in his career, Chandler developed a self-mocking tone that allowed Philip Marlowe both to say what Chandler couldn't get away with and to unsay what Marlowe couldn't get away with, in the act of saying it. That doesn't make "The Pencil" any better than it is, but it does mean that Marlowe's quasi-Byronic "romantic irony" was a needful wand, a proleptic aversion of disbelief, a preemption of scorn, a parrying of doubt. Marlowe anticipates the reader's rejection by voicing it first; he beats the doubter to the punch.

The visibility of these strategies in "The Pencil" is enhanced by the story's thin texture and some absurdities of execution. Anne Riordan's question, "'How come I'm still a virgin at twenty-eight?'" (347) is more pathetic than quaint and should have been addressed to the author, rather than the narrator.

Chandler's age and alcoholic despair had not entirely robbed him of his resources, however, for he still was able to voice his doubts through his puppet, Marlowe. Chandler's narrator himself dispenses the hints of dismissal provoked by his own assertions. When Marlowe says that Anne Riordan "went through the cigarette routine" (344), we can see that he has labelled as a cliché, the very cliché he brought up. Marlowe's confrontation with Charles Hickon leads him to an admission that could be Chandler's: "You have to lie a little once in a while in my business" (351). Hickon gives Marlowe "as dirty a look as he had in stock," as though he were an actor, and exits with what Marlowe calls a "blinding piece of repartee" (351). With such distancing repudiations and ironies, Marlowe puts his own story at arm's length. Marlowe's reaction to Hickon's dated tough-guy dialogue ("'Stay clean, tinhorn. Tin bends easy'"

[351]) makes him his own Marling.

Ikky tells Marlowe, "'Don't be a sap'" (354-55), but the story suggests that the narrator has already been one. His declaration in a slender paragraph that "they had shot the wrong man" (357) is itself wrong. His imagined police grilling prompts him to attribute to the hypothetical cops the clichés he voices. "Policeman's dialogue. It comes out of an old shoebox" (357). The old shoebox is likely to be the one in which the author stored his file cards. The tedium of tough-guy talk and pulp magazine plotting takes the form of Marlowe's lament over his office and job: "Why the hell hadn't I got myself a government job ten years ago?" (357-8). This complaint is not only a transposition of the author's wistfulness but also a reflection not so much on the job of the detective as on the job of writing the story of that job.

Marlowe's confrontation with Foster Grimes features threats and handguns— it's a scene from a bad movie or a pulp story, perhaps even one of Chandler's own. But since the triteness is overwhelming, Marlowe plays against it by pointing to the cliché during his own narrative of his own speech in his own scene: "'Look under the desk, Mr. Grimes. . . . A .45 slug can throw you back six feet. Even the movies learned that at last'" (362). The allusion to Hollywood is dizzying because Chandler aped the tough-guy voices and scenes of Hollywood and then became a source for screenplays and later a screenwriter himself. For Marlowe from the movies (as well as from radio and TV) to pose as superior to his own source and medium is a tricky diversion of the reader's instinctive rejection of the corny scene he's playing. The self-referentiality of the gesture is wrapped in its apparent rejection. That is to say, the formulaic detective gains credibility by sneering at his own formula, hoping to confuse the reader with a cloud of ink. As Marlowe says about Grimes, he could have said about the reader: "'I beat him to the punch'" (363).

The weakness of the story and Chandler's defensiveness are reasons to contemplate its nature and to ponder just how much those qualities are essentially Chandlerian. Approaching the climactic scene with Ikky, Marlowe, or rather Chandler, foists a self-referential episode that may be compared with ones in Chapter 13 of *The High Window* (1942) and Chapter 25 of *Playback* (1958). The hall of mirrors casts many reflections, including Don Quixote's visit to the print shop in Chapter 62, Volume 2, of the prototypical novel to which he gave his name and Mr. Dick's kite-flying in David Copperfield, "publishing" the pages of his Memorial, the inscribed substance of the kite itself, in Chapter 14 of that book about the making of a writer. But now it's Marlowe's turn to pick up a paperback such as the ones that are his own vehicles:

The paperback scared me so badly that I put two guns under my pillow. . . . Then I asked myself why I was reading this drivel when I could have been memorizing *The Brothers Karamazov*. Not knowing any good answers, I turned the light out and went to sleep. (364)

Paperback thrillers are a step up—one—from the pulp stories Chandler wrote in the thirties and, indeed, one step up from "The Pencil" itself, which was published as a pulp story. Marlowe attempts to distance himself from his own medium just as Chandler always claimed a distance from ordinary mysteries and certainly from the brutality of imitators such as James Hadley Chase and Mickey Spillane. The paperback is apparently lurid, but not "realistic"—as though the story we are reading were "realistic"! But if Marlowe would somehow rather read "this drivel" than memorize Dostoyevsky, then maybe our consciences are also relieved, for we are reading some drivel too. A further irony, of course, is that *The Brothers Karamazov* is, among other things, a lurid melodrama of sex and violence. Marlowe's perusal and evaluation of a paperback while he narrates a revival of the pulp story is an example of the quality known as *mise en abîme*.

When he catches up with Ikky, Marlowe tells him, "'You must think I'm dumb. . . . I am'" (364). He calls himself a "sucker" who "boobed off" (364-65). He is the "sap" he was warned not to be. But he is not as dumb as he pretends, because he has held out on the reader—he has solved the case but not disclosed it. His withheld reasoning is revealed in his confrontation with Ikky, in a denouement typical of Chandler in its rhetorical ponderousness and misuse of the paying customer, the reader, who must enjoy getting taken for a ride, for otherwise he wouldn't keep paying the fare.

Marlowe's forced recountal—"Ikky" doesn't need to hear what he already knows, but the reader does—is such a labored finish that Chandler again anticipates rejection. Where have we seen or heard this scene before? Marlowe's wit is a form of prolepsis, averting the reader from the groan of recognition, beating the doubter to the punch once again: "'The setup intrigued me,' I went on, debonair as Philo Vance in an S. S. Van Dine story and a lot brighter in the head" (365).

Even the false Ikky will claim to be tired of the explanation, once again trying to steer the reader away from an obvious truth: "'I don't know what the hell you're talking about. I just know it's too long'" (365). Marlowe's reply—"'Well, allow me to put it in English'" (365)—focuses our awareness on the clash of dictions that animates Chandler's verbal textures and also reinforces the sense of language as language that underlies the split consciousness and literariness of Chandler's doubly inverted slumming. "To put it in English" is how Marlowe's point is made but also how the author, not the narrator, wrote the story. In that story we find that "to put it in English" means sometimes to muddy the waters or even to deny them rather than to make things plainly clear. And, finally, "to put it in English" often meant, when Chandler wrote his tough-guy tales, to put it in American.

The climax of the story comes when Marlowe concludes his exposition of all the thinking he'd withheld from his audience and accuses Ikky of being an imposter. The real Ikky was the one he saw slain. Then regression to pulp violence dissolves all mental tension: "I shot the gun out of his hand. The gun in my coat pocket was small, but at that distance accurate. And it was one of my days to be accurate" (366). "Marlowe's" nervous awareness of his absurdity is covered up with the deadpan claim that he had one of those accurate days when he just couldn't miss—and rather conveniently timed it was, too. Since he's already noted the artificiality of it all, who are we to complain?

In a sense, Chandler had beat Marlowe to the punch years before. Keith Newlin (23-24) has identified this association—gunplay, a gun shot out of a hand or other such shots, the repudiation of this cliché as soon as it is stated—as a motif in several of Chandler's early stories written before Marlowe: "The Man Who Liked Dogs" (1936), "The Curtain" (1936), and "Bay City Blues" (1938). In that sense, "The Pencil" was for Chandler a recapitulation and a regression, but not a work to be avoided or ignored by us.

Back in L.A., sipping the bubbly with Anne Riordan, Marlowe admits that the deception of the false Ikky doesn't really make sense, which means that "The Pencil" is a shaky construction. Anne's quip says a lot about Marlowe the narrator, as distinguished from Marlowe the character: "'What I like about you, apart from your enormous personal charm, is that when you don't know an answer you make one up'" (367). This truth is voiced so that the story can contain and even restrict its own criticism. Chandler has handed to Anne one of the worst things we could say about his story, so that the story can deflect the thought by preempting its statement. Similarly, her injunction, "'Don't be a jerk all your life'" (367), applies better to Marlowe's narrative performances than it does to his personal behavior.

As a formulaic story, "The Pencil" is no better and no worse than it should be. But the insistence of the discourse upon its own fictive status transcends such considerations as "character" and "plot." Those hooks, baited to lure the unwary reader, aren't today half so attractive as the text's own sly hints at its own fictionality. Almost invisible because of its obviousness is the eponymous pencil itself. That writing instrument is the central image of a story that was itself *written*, though not, I think, with a pencil. Byron Preiss himself has described the "canary yellow pages, standard typewriter sheets cut in half, typed the long way, and triple spaced" (vii) in the UCLA Research Library, the Chandler typescripts with holograph corrections featuring a blue-on-yellow scheme that made for a "pretty" manuscript.

Nevertheless, "The Pencil" is a story about a symbol and image of writing, a writing instrument itself and one with which Marlowe literally writes. "The Pencil" was written, typed, typeset, and commercially published internationally and posthumously. But in that story Marlowe, after hearing "Ikky's" story about being pencilled, acts so as to cause himself to receive a "literal" pencil, which figuratively "pencils" him. When Marlowe rehashes the story of this story to Bernie Ohls, he pens or pencils the story of the pencil. "I wrote my name on a piece of paper and ran the pencil through it" (359). Marlowe's writing is deceptively obvious and obviously deceptive. He's signed his own name as though he were a Pinocchio, the puppet who's achieved autonomy. But the story he tells Ohls—a repetition of the story that his master had him tell us—is false, as well as a fiction within a fiction. "Ikky" wasn't Ikky, and Marlowe doesn't yet know why he was ever involved in the case, or if he does, he hasn't told us.

Furthermore, writing Marlowe's name and drawing a line through it when necessary was literally Raymond Chandler's self-defined job of work. It wasn't the Mob who "pencilled" either of the Ikky Rossens or Marlowe, it was Raymond Chandler who did so by writing the story. Chandler wrote Marlowe's name all the time and struck a line through it when he edited his material. And when Marlowe says that he did the same—wrote his name and pencilled through it as a vivid, though false, illustration for Ohls—it was Chandler who made the claim or wrote it. Only Chandler could do what Marlowe said he himself did: "sign" for Marlowe and cross through his name. Chandler did that every time he wrote a Marlowe novel. In his last story, he reified or literalized the illusion he regularly and professionally manipulated by *writing*—finally by transcribing words so that they could be mass produced through commercial publication and even translation and international distribution. A pencil can be more than an illusion, it can foster one. The pen is mightier than the sword because it can conquer the world. The pencil is mighty too, if less permanent in its impress, but conquest isn't always based on truth.

The wheels within wheels of Marlowe's fallacious story-within-the-story to Ohls and to his other, larger audience should not divert us from awareness of other such passages. We learn that Anne Riordan herself wrote nonsense about young love for the shiny magazines, not altogether unlike Raymond Chandler himself. When Marlowe tells her that "'Ikky has been pencilled,'" he adds, "'It's just bookkeeping to them'" (344). The authorial pun on "pencil" is extended to "bookkeeping," for Chandler had been both keeping the books and being kept by them for decades. Similarly, Marlowe's emphasis on the "word" is both natural and deceiving, when he says of Ikky, "There seemed to be a little gold in him somewhere—but little was the operative word" (349). Well might the word-man Marlowe use a word as a word.

All of the self-conscious playfulness, veering from the trite to the parody of triteness, illustrates the quality that Keith Newlin identified in 1984 in the title, *Hardboiled Burlesque: Raymond Chandler's Comic Style*. But going beyond burlesque, Chandler comically plays with self-reflexive allusions to modes of transmission and media of expression. As Bernie Ohls says, "'But they'll want to talk to you, Phil. They just love their tape recorders'" (359). Raymond Chandler just loved his dictaphone in La Jolla, as well.

When Marlowe receives a deceptive telegram, he gets another instance of fictional manipulation as well as another system of communication. And when Anne Riordan says, "'I don't like the pencil'" (360), she voices a statement that differs from her iteration in its self-referentiality: "*I don't like 'The Pencil'*." She goes on to comment on the case in terms that criticize the story that presents her: "'And I don't like the wrong man being killed. . . . You should never have touched it, Phil'" (360).

Later, Marlowe flips "the nicely sharpened pencil" at Foster Grimes, who's come to threaten and perhaps even kill this narrator who can't be silenced—by definition. His voice asserts a message and an understanding that's subverted by the story that presents them: "'It came to me by Special Delivery mail. No message, no return address. Just the pencil. Think I've never heard about the pencil, Mr. Grimes?'" (362).

Marlowe's further banter with Anne Riordan emphasizes again the pencil that threatens—while creating—Ikky and the detective. In their final showdown, those two wind up talking about a word as a word: *echelon* (365-66). Marlowe's confrontation with Ikky and his final recital are a miniature of the ritual ending of detective stories, one that is extended to further analysis back in L.A. with Anne. Their discussion of loose ends is in effect an analysis of the weaknesses of "The Pencil" itself, in a self-adjusting passage that crowns this product of a self-creating discourse.

Raymond Chandler kept playing the same old tricks to the end. Were they successful ones? That's a matter of taste, perhaps; but the work is still in print, still read, still cherished for its tone, and imitated *ad infinitum*: "The Rockford Files," various Woody Allen passages, *Dead Men Don't Wear Plaid, Who Killed Roger Rabbit?*, the Spenser books of Robert B. Parker, *City of Angels*, and so on. Philip Marlowe is always with us, and why shouldn't he be cloned or Chandler imitated, since Chandler so often cribbed from himself? The various recreations in Byron Preiss's collection are the sincerest forms of flattery, and it's nice to know that the homage to Chandler is up front and on the table. There is no rip-off, but rather an affectionate and knowing celebration.

One of the pasticheurs, the mystery novelist John Lutz, has spoken most pointedly in the afterword to his contribution to Preiss's collection:

The detective, observing, commenting, influencing, illuminating the clockwork of his corner of the world, is something like a novelist within a novel. It was Chandler who used this freedom and dimension to best advantage, lacing his perfectly balanced prose with wicked social insight, as well as beauty and poetry. Like a skilled photographer, he seemed to realize that the object in the lens is sometimes not as important as the light that falls on it. There are few genuine innovators in writing, and Chandler was one of them. Most of us who write this kind of fiction, whether we know it or not, or acknowledge it or not, emulate Raymond Chandler. I consider it an honor and a gesture of respect to emulate him consciously and publicly for this collection. (191)

Philip Marlowe was indeed "something like a novelist within a novel," as Lutz puts it, and was like one in a way in "The Pencil." Raymond Chandler's last story, like his early ones, played with the teeter-totter of credibility in a tale of violence and coincidence. The seesaw of reflexive ironies and the tension of elitist sensitivity projected through the sleaze of vulgar melodrama combine to forge a "literariness" from unlikely materials. The dynamic of the discourse, mocking its own substance and yet compelling attention, puts Raymond Chandler in the same league with Edgar Allan Poe in various of his performances and with Vladimir Nabokov in the playfulness and self-referentiality of his work. Chandler's stylishness retains much of its magic and music and preemptive trickiness, even in his last bow. The illusion foisted by the stream of discourse works its spell, even while calling attention, in postmodernist fashion to its own unreality. Neither Marlowe nor Chandler could have done it without the proverbial pencil.

REFERENCES

Chandler, Raymond. "The Pencil." In *Raymond Chandler's Philip Marlowe: A Centennial Celebration*, edited by Byron Preiss. New York: Perigee Books, 1990.
Lutz, John. [Afterword to] "Star Bright." In *Raymond Chandler's Philip Marlowe: A Centennial Celebration*, edited by Byron Preiss. New York: Perigee Books, 1990.
Marling, William H. *Raymond Chandler*. Boston: Twayne Publishers, 1986.
Newlin, Keith. *Hardboiled Burlesque: Raymond Chandler's Comic Style*. Madison, IN: Brownstone Books, 1984.
Preiss, Byron. "Foreword." In *Raymond Chandler's Philip Marlowe: A Centennial Celebration*, edited by Byron Preiss. New York: Perigee Books, 1990.

4

Film in Fiction: The Real and the Reel in Elmore Leonard

George Grella

Like many contemporary American novelists, Elmore Leonard apparently writes with the movies in mind; unlike most of his colleagues, however, he possesses more than a passing acquaintance or an academic knowledge of the subject. An experienced hand who rode the dangerous and dusty trails of the Western for many years, he has worked (and continues to work) in a variety of cinematic endeavors—his books and stories have provided the basis for a number of pictures, some of which he adapted himself; he has written educational films, original screenplays, and even novelizations (Geherin 7-10). He also differs from most of his colleagues in the use he makes of the art of cinema. Film serves him as much more than a goal, a profitable venue toward which his fiction points, a language into which it may later be translated; it is a guiding principle of composition, a rich source of devices and methods of plot, characterization, and narration. The motion pictures provide background and foreground, subject and object of many of his novels—several of them, in fact, are quite literally about film, are even in effect made out of film.

While acknowledging his originality, a great many of Leonard's readers have recognized his obvious connections with some of the great traditions of American crime fiction, which generally means invoking the names of Dashiell Hammett and James M. Cain. Perhaps eager to show off their own inside knowledge of crime and criminals, they praise the accuracy of his backgrounds, action, people and dialogue. Most of his background, of course, is the product of assiduous research, much of it farmed out to professionals.[1] Like Henry James, Ernest Hemingway, or John O'Hara, for example, he writes dialogue that looks on the page as if it were spoken by his people, which means that, authentic or not, it is, like all good dialogue, a highly stylized literary medium. Leonard's characters, who often dwell in the lower strata of society, may be criminals or cops, urban blacks or ethnics, or even practitioners of some special profession with its own jargon and therefore speak a slangy, colloquial, and frequently profane brand of contemporary American English. Some of the power of his work also derives from his adherence to the tough-guy tradition of relentless understatement; he presents the necessarily violent action of his novels—armed robberies, fights, beatings, shootings, murders—without metaphor or melodrama. All of his characteristic subjects and methods, along with his deadpan, wised-up, and often humorous tone, seductively invite readers into his narratives, flattering the audience with the unspoken assumption that they share the author's experience and his wry, cynical understanding of his people and places. The whole process convinces critics of the authenticity of the works by implicitly assuming they have been initiated into the exciting, dangerous, but somehow attractive milieu of cops and robbers, street thugs and slick thieves, sharp operators and dumb crooks.

In view of his use of the subject and techniques of cinema, however, Elmore Leonard might better be compared to other, more genteel writers. The presence of film in his work, in fact, suggests connections with some intellectually fashionable and perhaps more highly regarded contemporary novelists, those writers of what is sometimes called metafiction who often engage the labors of whole deconstruction companies of academic critics. In some of its richest and ripest manifestations, the complex cinematic influence inspires comparisons not only with Dashiell Hammett and James M. Cain but also with such famous experimental writers of the twentieth century as Pirandello, Calvino, Robbe-Grillet, Borges, and Nabokov. He may very well belong with those frequently discussed avant-garde artists who have extended the boundaries of their art in new directions, particularly through innovative handling of character and narrative.

In numerous interviews in various media, Elmore Leonard has asserted again and again that his novels depend, above all else, on the people who inhabit them.[2] According to the author, he dreams up his characters, who for him seem to be at least as real as they are for us, christens them with appropriate names, listens to them talk, and then allows them to make their own decisions. As in life, the people make things happen, acting and reacting, doing whatever it takes to move events into the complicated and sometimes crazy figures of his plots. Although those interviews indicate that he is a friendly and entirely unpretentious person, Leonard's comments imply a rather grand definition of the artist— cherished especially by artists themselves—in which the author assumes the role of God, breathing life into his creations and kindly providing them with an environment in which they can exercise their own free will. That free will not only allows them to choose whether to eat the forbidden fruit of the knowledge of good and evil but also enables them to conduct their lives; in other words, they go about the business of making his fiction. In a matter of speaking, Leonard's characters actually write his novels.

As he himself has helpfully pointed out, moreover, in most of those novels Leonard employs cinematic methods for stylistic purposes (Geherin 44 passim).

Released from the constraints of more orthodox exposition and generally minimizing the authorial voice, his novels tend to function by means of dialogue, scene change, and shifts in point of view, which not only places most of the burden of narrative upon the characters but also imitates the traditional methods of American movies. Leonard learned from classic Hollywood cinema the fictional equivalent of skillful filmmaking and film editing. He moves the angle of vision rapidly and frequently, for example, by cutting from character to character, point of view to point of view; the quick, smooth changes of scene, story, and people impart a Dickensian liveliness and daring to his novels, along with a paradoxically old-fashioned omniscience. The practice also accounts for the structure of happenstance and luck, the crazy pattern of change and coincidence that leads his novels in apparently random and sometimes fantastic directions, as the people move about, scheme, collide, act, and react. In Leonard's novels one thing always leads to another, but not necessarily in the most logical, predictable, or direct manner. Since his people propel the course of action, in effect creating the plots, the novels sometimes take on their own surreal logic, in which events follow one another in strange and wonderful ways; an accidental encounter may initiate an elaborate series of wildly connected actions, often involving a bizarre set of characters and generally culminating in violence. The various events of *La Brava* (1983) grow out of a chance meeting of all the principals at a mental health crisis center; though no one can know it at the time, Angela Nolan, an innocent bystander, is doomed once Detective Walter Kouza investigates the killing of a Haitian intruder in *Split Images* (1981); when Ernest Stickley tries to steal a 1973 Camaro in *Swag* (1976), he begins a course of action that leads to armed robbery, murder, and imprisonment and eventually to another novel as well; in *Get Shorty* (1990) the theft of Chili Palmer's leather jacket in Florida leads to Bo Catlett's death in California twelve years later; a live alligator dumped in a judge's backyard in *Maximum Bob* (1991) opens up a remarkable sequence of events involving a bizarre cast of characters, including a homicide detective, a probation officer, a drug-addicted dermatologist, a couple of ex-convicts, a former mermaid in a water show, and her spirit guide, a twelve-year-old slave girl who died in 1855. The oddly hallucinatory quality of Leonard's plot connections, the zestful nuttiness of his characterizations, both as Dickensian as his omniscience, remind us once again that film, of all the arts, most closely resembles dream.

Of course, if the characters are responsible for making the novels, then they are also responsible for the influence of cinema. Because they originally grow out of the author's mind, for one thing, and because both he and they have grown up in America, many of Leonard's characters, like many of us, discover in the movies a pattern for their words and deeds. They inhabit our world, they share our assumptions and experiences, they understand, perhaps without even knowing it, what Lionel Trilling, in a felicitous phrase, called the "culture's hum and buzz of implication" (200). As we all know, Hollywood is the capital city of all our dreams, which means that most of the people, good guys or bad, who populate Elmore Leonard's novels enjoy some relationship to the movies.

That relationship expresses itself in numerous and various ways, some obvious and more or less trivial. Like many authors, Leonard scatters allusions to well-known actors throughout his books; his characters think or talk about Humphrey Bogart, James Garner, Robert Mitchum, Warren Oates, and Harry Dean Stanton, for example, who serve to underline an attitude or even to point out a resemblance between someone in a book and a recognizable public person. Sometimes the books reflect his characters' concern with and knowledge of the cinema through some offhand references that provide a context for both observer and subject and tell us something about both. In *Split Images*, for example, Angela Nolan, who is a writer, observes Bryan Hurd on the witness stand: "She could see him firing a gun as she might see it in a dream or a movie. She saw it again in slow motion, looked at it closely and saw his expression the same as it was now. He fit the role of homicide lieutenant in a filmic way, look and manner adaptable to motion pictures" (39). His characters sometimes understand, as we all do, that when something particularly dramatic or melodramatic, remarkable or ridiculous, occurs, life starts to resemble art and remind us of the art we all share, the movies. When Barbara Mitchell's lawyer attempts to seduce her in *52-Pickup*, she experiences the common phenomenon of observing herself from outside the scene, thinking, "it was like a movie. Not a very good movie (87)," which describes a lot of moments in many lives. Leonard elaborates the process considerably in *City Primeval* (1980), which is subtitled *High Noon in Detroit*. Throughout the novel the police detective, Raymond Cruz, is frequently compared to the young Gregory Peck, which he understandably doesn't mind in the least, and himself recalls one of Peck's best-known Westerns, *The Gunfighter*, several times; the final shootout, which the detective actually initiates, consciously imitates a scene in that movie. Perhaps an act of homage to his work in the Western, Leonard's device seems awkward and artificial, but the book is redeemed by the presence of some fine Leonardesque characters, especially the kill-crazy Clement Mansell, the Oklahoma Wildman.

More functionally and meaningfully, movies provide an essential item in some of Leonard's books, mostly as devices of the criminals or pivot points around which the plots revolve. In *Stick* (1983) a dubious Hollywood producer named Leo Firestone tries out a ridiculous movie idea on a bunch of drug dealers and crooked investors with money to launder and taxes to evade. In the early thriller *52-Pickup* the villains film their murder of a young woman and screen it in a porno palace called the Imperial Art Theater in order to blackmail Harry Mitchell; as the killer who narrates the movie dreams of making a high-class skin flick, he displays an awareness of film terminology, commenting on establishing shots, zooms, closeups, cuts, camera angles, and point of view. In an age when the magic of technology has made every man his own pornographer, Leonard also exploits the film-related device of videotape. For Robbie Daniels, the millionaire psychopath of *Split Images*, much of the fun of killing people lies in photographing the act for his later viewing pleasure. His memorable sidekick, the former Detroit cop Walter Kouza, shoots hours of tape of Robbie's intended victim, a Latin American drug dealer with his beautiful mistress, to prepare for the climactic event and record it for his boss's recollection in tranquillity. Although Leonard typically surrounds the whole business of Kouza's difficulties in videotaping with a good deal of humor, his taping of the ultimate act, the killing of Angela Nolan, is deadly serious and leads to Bryan Hurd's revenge against both Kouza and Daniels.

Most important and perhaps most surprising, in some of his more recent fiction Leonard goes beyond cinema as a device, employing it in some daring, risky, even avant-garde ways as a key to structure and meaning. The most consciously and artfully cinematic of all of Leonard's novels are one from several years ago, *La Brava* (1983), and the more recent *Get Shorty* (1990). In both works, the characters pursue their mostly sinister designs and construct their various plans—which turn out to be the plots of the books, of course—according to what is sometimes called a scenario. Inspired by film, they pattern their actions after the movies; in fact, they quite literally make movies. The characters not only copy particular actions and statements but also learn from the cinema their various manipulations, deceptions, and betrayals; they then create their own versions—writing, directing, producing, casting, and in effect performing in their own movies. Dickens's David Copperfield aspires, like all of us, to be the hero of his own life; Leonard's characters aspire to be the Orson Welles of theirs.

In the first book, the memory of a particular movie within a particular genre—appropriately, film noir—inspires a plot involving extortion and murder. In the second, which not coincidentally takes place in Hollywood, everybody, also not at all coincidentally, is writing a screenplay and directing a movie. In *La Brava*, Jean Shaw, a former movie star, with the assistance of a brutal thug from the Florida swamps, concocts an elaborate fake extortion plot to swindle her elderly friend and sometime protector Maurice Zola out of $600,000. Jean, who always played the bad girl, the spider woman as she puts it, in tough, sexy little melodramas called *Deadfall*, *Nightshade*, and *Let It Ride*, patterns her plan after *Obituary*, in which she starred with Victor Mature, Henry Silva, Shepperd Strudwick, and Elisha Cook, Jr. (it sounds like a composite of all the films noirs we've ever seen). All the important characters in the book come to play new versions of those characters in the original movie, which of course is a Leonard invention in the first place.

As the plot gathers momentum, Joe La Brava, the former Secret Service agent, begins to recognize the movie that inspires the real-life action. A number of other film-related devices, however, complicate what at first seems a rather simple situation. To begin with, La Brava, who is attempting to make a career as a photographer and beginning to find his own style and even some success, possesses a special sensitivity to the picture he sees unfolding before and around him. More important, he has also nurtured a passion for Jean Shaw ever since he saw her in *Obituary* when he was twelve; and their brief affair, which should be a natural culmination of his adolescent sexual fantasies, only serves to draw him into her movie. The aesthetic and physical passions coincide and combine with a certain nostalgia; for a while, as a result, Joe La Brava finds himself participating in Jean Shaw's plot, duped like all the other characters in the original movie and in the novel itself, playing the sincere, conscientious boyfriend betrayed by the familiar dark lady of film noir.

The novel employs so many cinematic allusions, including many to particular scenes, characters, and lines in any number of movies that it is difficult to separate the actual from the invented titles. La Brava himself can never fully accept Jean Shaw the person without reference to her screen roles and wonders constantly, even in their most intimate moments, whether she is sincere or merely acting. The blurring of film and real life also introduces a number of conversations about Jean Shaw's movies and about cinema in general, which leads to some quite unusual subjects for a novel ostensibly devoted to extortion, betrayal, murder, and detection. La Brava may be Leonard's most visually oriented novel, more detailed than any other in its attention to the light, the coloring, the look, the quite literally picturesque quality of Miami. The book frequently pauses for visual analysis, some informed talk about film, photography, and painting, about the differences between color and black-and-white visions, some of them naturally generated by Jean Shaw's old films; astonishingly, the book's cinematic inspiration and discussions suggest that it may really be Leonard's *Künstlerroman*, a novel about art, artists, and even art criticism.

Joe La Brava is not the only photographer in this novel in which everybody makes pictures of one kind or another. Maurice Zola, who is a former photographer as well as a retired bookie, real estate investor, and vaguely shady entrepreneur, opens the book by aggressively pushing La Brava's work to a gallery owner. He places his friend in exalted company, comparing him to "'Diane Arbus . . . Duane Michaels, Danny Lyon, Winogrand, Lee Friedlander . . . Walker Evans'" (7). While Jean Shaw manipulates both him and her accomplice Richard Nobles in her movie plot, La Brava himself enjoys a second sexual connection with a bouncy painter named Fanny Kaufman, who is actually the appropriate partner for him, an involvement that extends and complicates the themes of art and sex. Fanny dreams of doing a thirty-foot painting of the old streamlined pastel, Art Deco Miami hotels and wonders why La Brava sticks to black-and-white photography. Ironically, he replies that he "feel[s] safer" in that medium. Of course, black and white is actually the dangerous medium of Jean Shaw's pictures.

The art criticism applies to both motion pictures and still photography, so that the novel occasionally resembles far more ambitious sorts of fiction. In one scene that Leonard later duplicates several times in *Get Shorty*, Franny and Jean discuss *Let It Ride*, one of Jean's movies, their dialogue set off on the page as if they were characters speaking in a film script. Somehow Leonard gets away with a conversation that sounds like two sophisticated film critics analyzing the latest trendy masterpiece from some foreign shore. Franny talks about the "lighting and composition," which Jean calls "the ominous *mise en scène*," and suggests that "expressionistic realism" implies psychosis in the movie. La Brava himself quotes the things people say about his photographs, which sound very much like the artier sorts of reviews of any creative work these days; one of the sentences helps explain the novel—"The aesthetic sub-text of his work is the systematic exposure of artistic pretension" (101).[3] Joe La Brava's response suggests something of Leonard's own reaction to pretentious criticism: "'I thought I was just taking pictures.'"

At a different point in the novel, La Brava thinks seriously about a statement he reads in a photographic journal that in a sense explains not only his own preoccupation with Jean Shaw but perhaps also the temporary deception she works upon him. An article discussing the differences between photographs and moving pictures expresses the complex nostalgia that motivates their relationship with her—"a still picture is more powerful than a motion picture, more memorable, [the] images from movies that stay with you are reasonably still" (140). When Jean Shaw's complicated plot finally unravels, as we know it must, and La Brava helps tie up the loose ends, he manages to freeze that last memorable still picture with a word and an expression he's been thinking about for most of the book. He sums up everything—his past, his adolescent crush, her movies, their sexual entanglement, her manipulation and betrayal, his rescuing her from her own scheme—with a self-consciously fake-tough final line right out of a Jean Shaw flick: "'Swell,'" followed by a "nice smile: Maybe a little weary but still a nice one. Why not?" (283). He has managed to conclude her movie with his own still photograph; his art triumphs, more or less, over hers.

The Leonard book most fully devoted to film is the Hollywood novel, *Get Shorty*, a remarkably modernist thriller about a gangster who decides he wants to make a movie. Chili Palmer, a loan shark and movie buff, travels to California from Florida via Las Vegas on an increasingly convoluted mission. Initially searching for a deadbeat who faked his own death so that his wife could receive a big insurance settlement, Chili also goes after a man named Harry Zimm to call in a gambling marker. As it happens, Harry Zimm is a Hollywood producer responsible for such masterpieces of the cinema as *Slime Creatures* and *Grotesque, Part Two*, so instead of threatening him in the time-honored kneebreaking tradition, Chili tries out his idea for a film on him; the script, naturally, is based on the mission that brought Chili to California in the first place. The extraordinary complications in this most complicated novel grow out of the constant dialectic between Chili's life and the movie he wants to make. He not only regards some areas of his past experience as cinematic, but also begins to think about everything he does as cinema, coming to realize that he is acting in a movie whose outcome he doesn't yet know. He experiments with ideas, decisions, paths of action, all the time seeing them as elements in a movie—when he thinks of what might have happened if he'd taken his quarry's wife to Las Vegas, "he realized he was thinking of it as a movie again . . . but seeing new possibilities, getting the woman Fay into the story more" (101) and inevitably begins to ponder casting for the movie of his life, with Robert DeNiro playing himself. The ideas, of course, in their turn influence everything else that happens in what Chili, despite all evidence to the contrary, persists in believing is real life.

The cinematic possibilities don't stop with the realization that the characters are making up the movie that constitutes the life they live in the novel. Harry Zimm wants to make his own movie, *Mr. Lovejoy*, which competes in several ways with the one he, Chili, and everybody else seem to be inhabiting; but a couple of his creditors, slick drug dealers laundering money through the industry, impede his production. One of them, Bo Catlett, a tough smoothie who becomes Chili's nemesis, goes so far as to tinker with the *Mr. Lovejoy* script in the time-honored and much-despised fashion of all movie money people everywhere; he and Chili even sit around reading the script of Harry's movie, several pages of which appear in the novel. They discuss the ethic and aesthetic of film in general, the sacred concept of motivation that Hollywood people love to toss around so blithely, and the meaning of *Mr. Lovejoy*:

"'What you don't understand,' Catlett said, 'is what the movie is saying. You live clean, the shit gets taken care of somehow or other. That's what the movie's about.'"
"'You believe that?'"
"'In movies, yeah. Movies haven't got nothing to do with real life.'" (141-42)

Chili wants to disagree with Catlett's theory in part because he would like his own movie to work out, as Harry tells him; there's no good guy in the script he's writing and living—nobody is going to identify or sympathize with a shylock, which of course also presents a problem in Leonard's novel. In order to have his script work out, Chili must become at least minimally admirable, a status he achieves through some remarkably agile manipulation, some resourceful action, and some very quick thinking. He makes love to Karen Flores, who was a great scream queen in Harry's films and is Harry's former lover and an ex-wife of Michael Weir, the actor Chili wants to play himself. He deftly extricates himself from a confrontation with a Mafia enemy bent on revenge and with the help of a former stuntman defeats Bo Catlett in a situation copied, naturally, from a movie. (Karen Flores has already saved his life by doing her best horror-flick scream.) That trick, together with his final dismissal of the big movie star who's been stringing Chili along on his script, helps to make him something of a success. Even as his story ends Chili seems still in the process of becoming the hero of his own movie.

In its general and particular satire of the whole movie industry, much of the book recalls a tradition of Hollywood fiction that includes works as different as *The Day of the Locust*, *What Makes Sammy Run?* and even *The Loved One*. It provides inside information on investing, studio meetings, negotiations with stars, and deals with agents, as well as the usual Leonardesque recording of the specialized speech of a distinct subculture. No doubt inspired by Leonard's own personal knowledge, the book suggests something of the author's revenge on Hollywood. Judging by the character, appearance, and behavior of the actor Michael Weir, some specific elements apparently derive from Leonard's experience with Dustin Hoffman.[4] At a relatively early point in the book, quite soon after the quoted remarks enlightening Chili on the subject of what movies are about, Catlett instructs him in the business of screenwriting, no doubt echoing any number of story conferences Elmore Leonard participated in, listening to brazen morons tampering with scripts.

"You asking me," Catlett said, "do I know how to write down words on a piece of paper? That's what you do, man, you put down one word after the other as it comes into your head. It isn't like having to learn how to play the piano, like you have to learn notes. You already learned in school how to write, didn't you? I *hope* so. You have the idea and you put down what you want to say. Then you get somebody to add in the commas and shit where they belong if you aren't positive yourself. Maybe fix up the spelling where you have some tricky words. There people do that for you. Some, I've seen scripts where I *know* words weren't spelled right and there was hardly any commas in it. So I don't think it's too important. You come to the last page you write in 'Fade out' and that's the end, you're done." (143)

After all the setups, angles, shots, and sequences in the novel and the many pages of script, and all the rewrites, all the discussions of casting, acting and production, and especially all the inside dope on the movie business, *Get Shorty* ends with the same ambiguity as the script of *Mr. Lovejoy*, so that Harry's and Chili's movies once again coincide. When Chili and Harry participate in a meeting at a studio and discuss their movie with Michael Weir, Harry thinks they will be talking about making his movie, but in fact the subject is Chili's movie. When the whole enterprise dissolves because of the star's mercurial temperament and undependability, Chili insults the annoying poseur, finally making sense of the book's cryptic title and setting up the indeterminate, ambiguous, open-ended conclusion of the novel. Like both Harry's and Chili's movies, it never really reaches a proper resolution. It's another movie that doesn't finally get made. Chili's final thoughts, the last sentence of *Get Shorty*, sum up all the strands of action and meaning in the novel and the films: "Fuckin endings, man, they weren't as easy as they looked" (292).

NOTES

1. See, for example, Gregg Sutter, "Researching Elmore Leonard's Novels, Part I," *Armchair Detective* (Winter 1986), 4-19.

2. For a partial list of interviews with the author, see Geherin, 148.

3. As David Geherin points out (133), the quotation actually comes from a review of Leonard in—where else?—*The Village Voice*.

4. The brief paragraph from Geherin (113) is worth quoting in its entirety: "Leonard also spent a great deal of time on a frustrating succession of rewrites of the *La Brava*

screenplay to satisfy Dustin Hoffman, who finally approved the script and agreed to star in the film. However, the project fell apart when Hoffman later became involved in a dispute with one of the producers, Cannon Films. He broke his own contract and backed out of the project."

REFERENCES

Geherin, David. *Elmore Leonard*. New York: Continuum, 1989.

Leonard, Elmore. *City Primeval: High Noon in Detroit*. New York: Arbor House, 1980.

_____. *52-Pickup*. London: Pan Books, 1977.

_____. *Get Shorty*. New York: Delacorte Press, 1990.

_____. *La Brava*. New York: Arbor House, 1983.

_____. *Maximum Bob*. New York: Delacorte Press, 1991.

_____. *Split Images: A Novel*. New York: Arbor House, 1981.

_____. *Swag*. New York: Delacorte Press, 1976.

Most, Glenn W. "Elmore Leonard: Splitting Images." In *The Sleuth and the Scholar*, edited by Barbara A. Rader and Howard G. Zettler, 101-10. New York: Greenwood Press, 1988.

Trilling, Lionel. "Manners, Morals, and the Novel." In *The Liberal Imagination*. Garden City, NY: Doubleday, 1957.

5

"Aggravating the Reader":
The Harlem Detective Novels
of Chester Himes

Gary P. Storhoff

In Chester Himes's first detective novel, *A Rage in Harlem* (1957), perhaps the most memorable passage is how Goldy meets his end. In many ways, Goldy is the most delightful character in the novel: A con artist, he makes his living dressed as a nun, selling tickets to heaven; and although everyone believes he is a woman, he dutifully visits his wife every weekend. Though successful at his calling, he supplements his income as a stoolie for the "famous Harlem detective team of Coffin Ed Johnson and Grave Digger Jones" (44), to whom he also preaches the Gospel. Throughout the first half of the novel, Himes invites us to see much of the action from his comic perspective. However, Goldy ultimately oversteps his bounds of petty criminality when he becomes involved in the search for the lost gold and in so doing becomes entangled with *real* gangsters. Enraged as much by Goldy's transvestism as by his stooling, Jodie, the psychopath with a switchblade, forces Goldy to the pavement, jerks "Goldy's head back against the pressure of his knee, and cut[s] Goldy's taut black throat from ear to ear, straight down to the bone" (105). At that point in the novel, Himes expresses the true "rage in Harlem," the rage that he shares with other African Americans:

Goldy's scream mingled with the scream of the locomotive as the train thundered past overhead, shaking the entire tenement city. Shaking the sleeping black people in their lice-ridden beds. Shaking the ancient bones and the aching muscles and the t.b. lungs and the uneasy foetuses of unwed girls. Shaking plaster from ceilings, mortar from between the bricks of the building walls. Shaking the rats between the walls, the cockroaches crawling over kitchen sinks and leftover food; shaking the sleeping flies hibernating in lumps like bees behind the casings of the windows. Shaking the fat, blood-filled bedbugs crawling over black skin. Shaking the fleas, making them hop. Shaking the sleeping dogs in their filthy pallets, the sleeping cats, the clogged toilets, loosening the filth. (105)

It is also the reader who is "shaken."

Whatever his moral status, Goldy has been a center of reference in the novel, and his horrifying death violently deprives the reader of a focal narrative perspective. Goldy was capable of negotiating the treacherous world of Harlem successfully, gulling not only the residents (epitomized, perhaps, by his trusting brother Jackson), but also the small-time crooks who presumably reign supreme in Harlem before the novel's plot begins. Himes invites the reader to accord the renegade Goldy respect—and therefore narrational intelligence—not because of Goldy's moral position or intellect but simply because of Goldy's fertile flexibility, his willingness to employ ingenious disguises and stratagems to accomplish his version of the American success story. (It is unsurprising that in Hollywood's sanitized production of *A Rage in Harlem*, Goldy is the courageous hero who survives, rescues Jackson, wins the gold, and lives happily ever after, presumably giving up his life of crime in memory of his much-loved, recently deceased mother.) The faithless Imabelle, apparently seeing in Jackson a man who will bring her closer to Jesus Christ, marries him, after serious doubts that she really deserves him. With Goldy's death in the novel, however, the reader is adrift in a bizarre fictive world without narrational guidance; if even the most amoral character is brutally murdered, what expectations can the reader (even a detective-novel reader) entertain? Goldy's death scene epitomizes Himes's aesthetic method in his Harlem detective stories. Chester Himes uses the detective genre throughout his career to "shake up" the reader, to expose and then radicalize the social and political ideologies concealed by the detective fiction form.

Peter Rabinowitz and H. Bruce Franklin have already argued that Himes's use of the detective novel genre is thematically subversive, the content of his fiction controlled by his radical political principles. For both Rabinowitz and Franklin, the issue centers on Detectives Coffin Ed and Grave Digger acting on both sides of the fence—African Americans who enforce a racially oppressive system. In contrast to more "humanistic" critics such as Stephen Milliken, Edward Margolies, Raymond Nelson, and Robert E. Skinner,[1] Rabinowitz contends that Himes's fiction is largely directed by political ideas. "It's easy," Rabinowitz argues, "to see how being on both sides of the oppressive power structure portrayed in these books would produce the smoldering rage that marks Coffin Ed in particular, a rage that's ready to erupt at the slightest provocation" (25). Franklin writes: "Himes's Black killer-detectives protect the people of Harlem by enforcing upon them the law and order of white capitalist America, doing this with a brutal and often literally blind violence their white colleagues can no longer employ with impunity, often committing more crimes than they solve. They embody what they represent, the ultimate stage of social disorder masquerading as order" (224). A thematic analysis of Himes's work, for both Franklin and Rabinowitz, reveals Himes's political revolt against a white power structure.

But the Rabinowitz-Franklin thesis can be carried a step further: That Himes's rage is not confined within his characters, but is instead directed clearly at the aesthetic sensibilities of the reader—in essence, a white, middle-class reader—and that his work mounts a formidable assault on the detective form itself. "Genres," writes Frederic Jameson, "are essentially literary *institutions*, or social contracts between a writer and a specific public" (106). Thus, when Himes deliberately violates the conventions of the form and averts intentionally the reader's most elementary expectations (e.g., Himes's choice to destroy brutally a reasonably reliable narrative focus in Goldy), he perforce voids Jameson's sense of literary conventions as the "social contract." As such, the Harlem of Himes becomes a model interrogation of the hidden assumptions of popular literature, his radicalism expressed not only thematically (as Rabinowitz and Franklin argue) but also formally, by exposing the structural premises of the genre. His radicalized political principles, his racial militancy, and his contempt for the middle-class ethos of hard work and propriety, all have *formal* consequences in his detective fiction as well as thematic relevance.

Himes himself remarked, "I want these people [his white readership] just to take me seriously. I don't care if they think I'm a barbarian, a savage, or what they think; just think I'm a serious savage" (Williams 314). Explicit in Himes's remark is a distrust of his readership, verging on hostility; a vision of himself as a teller of a tale that *assaults* the reader so that finally he or she begins to *hear* what he is trying to say. Born in Missouri in 1909 and raised in the South, Himes was unprepared for the racism he encountered in the North, when he began college at Ohio State University. Though he had been identified by standardized testing as brilliant, the Jim Crow regulations at Ohio State eventually led him into crime; at the age of nineteen, he was sentenced for armed robbery to twenty-five years in the Ohio State Penitentiary (he served seven years). He came to maturity in prison, witnessing the brutality of convicts and guards and the terrible Easter fire in 1930, when over 330 convicts were killed. In the first volume of his autobiography, *The Quality of Hurt*, Himes writes that he survived his prison experience by rage: "I had such violent seizures of rage that I made men twice my size quake with fright. In my fits of insensate fury I would have smashed the world, crushed it in my hands, kicked down the universe" (62). However, he succeeded in channelling his rage into his literature and began writing in prison. In the second volume of his autobiography, *My Life of Absurdity* (1976), he writes, "I had come to a final decision a long time ago when I was in prison that I was going to live as long as possible to aggravate the white race" (13).

The aggravation he intends to inflict is produced in his manipulation of the detective fiction genre, a commodity consumed by a middle class eager for vicarious thrills but not for the kind of shock Himes prepares. (Unsurprisingly, his novels sold mainly in France; they were never well received in America and until very recently have been out of print.) His "serious savagery," then, is both obvious (in his depiction of ghastly crime) and subtly implied in his aggression against his reader—a fact that profoundly affects his form.

As many writers have shown, the detective thriller is an essentially conservative vehicle. Activating a detached protagonist, assigned to redeem a fallen world (W. H. Auden's guilty vicarage) and to restore—at least partially—an original but unacknowledged innocence, the genre is notable for evoking the unconscious anxieties of its readership, then allaying and reassuring the reader by "solving" the crime, thereby eliminating the source of the fictive world's social dislocation. Even in the hard-boiled school, where the concept of crime is more pervasive than in the classic English detective novel and where the detective's solution is much less definitive, we have at least a protagonist who embodies a highly individualistic "code"—the integrated and individualized Self against the dirty World (one thinks of Hammett's work ethic in the Continental Op stories or of Chandler's chivalric heroism). The Marxist critic Stephen Knight in *Form and Ideology in Crime Fiction*, for example, surveys the literary history of the detective novel plot to discover a socioeconomic subtext. For Knight, the typical crime throughout the genre's history inevitably constitutes a generalized threat to middle-class privilege; and the detective, in asserting the effectiveness of bourgeois individualism, solves the crime and thereby reassures the reader. Because the detective novel continually demonstrates the social system preserving itself, Knight theorizes, the reader's catharsis occurs when his/her latent anxiety about social instability is relieved. The detective novel becomes a political anodyne.

But for a political radical like Chester Himes, Knight's generic descriptions, for the most part accurate for writers from Edgar Allan Poe to P. D. James, are unsatisfactory. Himes offers his readers none of the commonplace structural features of either the classic English detective novel or the American hard-boiled variety. The "social contract" that Jameson assumes as the basis of genre-formation is continuously violated. In Himes's novels, the initial crimes, whatever they are, seldom generate the novels' plots; the bizarre complications seem largely irrelevant to the texts' central action; the barbarity of the violence disrupts rather than underscores any main theme; the detectives, their own self-serving comments to the contrary, wage war not to maintain a political system, help their people, or sustain an impersonal code but mainly to consolidate their own power base in Harlem: "Colored folks didn't respect colored cops. But they respected big shiny pistols and sudden death. It was said in Harlem that Coffin Ed's pistol would kill a rock and that Grave Digger's would bury it" (*A Rage in Harlem* 49). Most important of all, Himes's texts offer no catharsis for the reader, no imagined solution and eventual release from a world of brutality. Instead, we as readers are immersed in savage crime, and we are forced to sense a collective, sociopolitical responsibility for its perpetuation.

The most important way Himes destablilizes the detective form is in his creation of his two detectives, Coffin Ed and Grave Digger. Himes himself is misleading on his account of the creation of Digger and Ed: "When I went into . . . the detective story field, I was just imitating all the other American detective story writers, other than the fact that I introduced various new angles which were my own. . . . I just made the faces black, that's all" (Williams 313). Those "various new angles" represent the real issue of his work, for the two detectives mark a dramatic departure from convention. From the very beginning of Himes's career as a detective novelist, the two represent no real cohesive force for social order, no demonstrable source of rationality. Other critics of Himes have made much of the fact that superficially the two detectives evolve as Himes becomes more practiced in the genre—that in *A Rage in Harlem* the two take bribes, for example, but in later novels they do not or that the detectives occasionally make comments such as the following: "What hurts me most about this business is the attitude of the public toward cops like me and Digger. Folks just don't want to believe that what we're trying to do is make a decent peaceful place for people to live in, and we're going about it the best way we know how. People think we enjoy being tough, shooting people and knocking them in the head" (*The Heat's On*, 1966, 174). But such special pleading can hardly convince us of "their genuine love for their people, their altruistic hopes for communal peace and decency" (Nelson 174). Nor will it serve Himes to describe them as "antiheroes . . . fantastical, Herculean figures, native sons struggling with sensational and peculiarly indigenous forms of American violence in an effort to protect their culture from chaos" (Muller 88).

The detectives are neither misunderstood altruists nor guardians of African-American culture: To assert that they are diminishes Chester Himes and robs him of his political radicalism. Instead, we have an overwhelming sense of the detectives' complicity in the phantasmagoric world they inhabit, of their eager willingness to participate in a Hobbesian world where monsters prey on weaker monsters. In *The Heat's On*, for instance, Ed sacrifices a naked, tied-up woman, cutting a line six inches across her throat, then shows her in a mirror what he has done: "He knew that he had gone beyond the line; that he had gone outside of human restraint; he knew that what he was doing was unforgivable. But he didn't want any more lies" (145). Although Digger is somewhat more reserved in his brutality, he will also unleash deadly force, as when he almost beats an unarmed pimp to death in *The Real Cool Killers* (1959). It is true that Digger sometimes restrains Ed's ferocity, but much more often he cooperates with Ed or initiates the violence, as in *The Crazy Kill*, when they "interrogate" a villain by handcuffing his feet together, hanging him from a door, and—using their feet in his armpits—bear down on him until he gives the information they want. Knowing that Himes himself was the victim of similar torture by Chicago police in the 1920s further problematizes the detectives' "heroism."

Furthermore, at the end of Himes's career as a detective novelist, he planned in an uncompleted manuscript to have the detectives fight each other during a racial war: "I began writing a book called *Plan B*, about a real black revolution in which my two black detectives split up and eventually Grave Digger kills Coffin Ed to save the cause" (*My Life of Absurdity* 360). *Plan B* was eventually put aside and never finished. No English publication of *Plan B* exists; but to imagine, for example, Sherlock Holmes plotting to kill Dr. Watson because of a political dispute will give an impression of the extremity of Himes's decision to wrench the form.

An even more important structural disruption of the detective novel is Himes's refusal to abide by the norms of narrative chronology. Perhaps the most teleological of all popular fiction, the detective novel usually adheres to Aristotelean conventions of time, which are linear, incremental, and fundamentally purposive: A crime is committed to begin the plot, the detective assembles evidence throughout the plot's middle, and at the plot's end he reveals the solution. An embedded assumption is that some moments, in discrete and measurable units, are more important or significant than others, as when the detective makes a "break" in the case or when an especially important clue (as opposed to a "red herring") is revealed to the reader. The plot is inevitably forward-moving; flash-backs are utilized, but only as episodes collateral to the denouement, to support or rationalize the narrative's closure.

But in Himes's texts, the reader's effort to delineate a conventional plot is usually frustrated. (Often, this is attributed to Himes's "carelessness" in his use of the form.) The "beginning" of his narrative quickly dissolves into a mass of past violence, grief, and horror. Almost immediately, plot chronology yields to an entirely different time pattern: Cyclical rather than linear, since we know that one crime simply repeats an earlier one; accretive rather than incremental, since the text's power relies on the cumulative force of violence; and encompassing rather than disjunctive, since we are usually distracted from "important" moments (i.e., clues) and are immersed in daily, "ordinary" events of criminality. It is extraordinarily difficult for the reader to reassemble retrospectively the logically sequacious order of clues and evidence, leading inexorably to a resolution, for the author continually intervenes with increasingly bizarre acts of violence.

Himes's experiments with violence to disrupt chronological sequencing recall the work of William Faulkner, whom Himes calls in *My Life of Absurdity* "my secret mentor. I could lift scenes straight out of Faulkner," Himes writes, "and put them down in Harlem and all I had to change was the scene" (169). Faulkner, of course, was himself interested in experimenting with the formal properties of detective fiction. Certain scenes throughout Himes's work correlate with Faulkner's Southern Gothic: In *A Rage in Harlem*, for example, Goldy's corpse falls out of a hearse and rolls into public view, much like a corresponding scene in *Sanctuary*, where Red's corpse falls out of the casket and rolls on the floor. More significant, Himes's purpose, like Faulkner's, is to occlude textual meaning, to keep the text open with inconclusive meanings by shattering narrative chronology, not only in flashbacks but in ways that shock, confuse, and deceive. Neither Faulkner nor Himes creates narrators who are thoroughly reliable; thus, like Faulkner's work, Himes's texts leave readers on their own to devise meanings—none of which seems entirely adequate to the narrative. If Faulkner deconstructs the historical novel, surely Himes deconstructs the detective novel.

One gruesome example illustrates Himes's deconstruction of the conventional narrative principles of detective fiction. Near the end of *The Heat's On*, Coffin Ed and Grave Digger are close to solving the case by pursuing leads that seem tenuous at best because of several narrative disruptions in the plot's chronology. Then, Himes abruptly interrupts their activities. The sinister Sister Heavenly takes her dog Sheba for a walk. Sister Heavenly, "one of the devil's mistresses," deals in narcotics, some of which she has concealed in her pets' rectums. (Surrounded by her menagerie, she also keeps rabbits, for the same purpose.) An explosion has accidentally destroyed Sister Heavenly's house, along with her considerable cache of narcotics, and she is forced to retrieve a supply from her pet Sheba. She checks into a flop house, kills and disembowels the dog, searches in its entrails for heroin, and, overcome by the stench and gore, vomits twice into its empty carcass. We then return to Digger and Ed as they disentangle clues—but with what interest? Within the context of the hegemonic, dominant culture Himes wrote against, these kinds of narrational disruptions are more than distracting—they are scandalous, indecorous, vulgar, and offensive.

These random interruptions of mayhem have led some readers to discover Himes's symbolic statements. For instance, in *All Shot Up* (1960), Digger and Ed are pursuing a tire thief who they hope will give them important information. The thief attempts to escape on his motorcycle, but because Ed has shot out his tire, he collides with a truck carrying sheets of steel. He is decapitated by a steel sheet, and the truck driver sees "a man without a head passing on a motorcycle . . . and a stream of blood flowing back in the wind" (88-89). This scene, it is suggested, symbolizes "bodies that have lost their essential consciousness, their essential humanity" (Nelson 170). Such readings are not so much "wrong" as they are utterly foreign to the experience of reading a Himes novel. Although such different writers as Dorothy Sayers (with her bells in *The Nine Tailors*) and Hammett (with *The Glass Key* or *The Maltese Falcon*) encourage the lay reader to speculate on the text's symbolic nuances, Himes seems almost to forbid this kind of interpretive reading.

Traversing his texts is a kind of coding that mocks the reader who wants his "lesson"—what Dennis Porter in another context might call his "moral education" (39)—served elegantly and neatly. For example, *All Shot Up* features the decapitation described above and a man stabbed through the head with a huge hunting knife; but the novel's last words are from a telegram sent to a swindler: "*Crime doesn't pay*" (170). Susan Sontag, in her essay "Against Interpretation," argues that occasionally interpretation itself "doesn't pay": "In some cultural contexts, interpretation is a liberating act. It is a means of revising, of transvaluing, of escaping the dead past. In other cultural contexts, it is reactionary, cowardly, stifling" (7). Surely, in Himes one must interpret with Sontag's admonition in mind. To interpret Himes's work moralistically is to denude him of his revolutionary energy and to distort his achievement in a genre known for its conservative, even reactionary bias.

Conventions of narrative closure are also upended by Himes. However provisional the sense of ending in *Red Harvest* with martial law prevailing in Poisonville, at least Hammett does give the reader a sense of resolution. Himes seldom does. Many of his novels end with criminals going free, sometimes because it is necessary (as in *Cotton Comes to Harlem*, 1965), or sometimes because the detectives' power is severely limited (as in *All Shot Up*). "Happy endings" are savagely parodied: Both *A Rage in Harlem* and *The Real Cool Killers* end improbably with presumptive marriages. The reader coming to Himes expecting reassurance and resolution must sense the author's not-so-playful derision. Many critics see Himes's last novel, *Blind Man with a Pistol* (1969), as his renunciation of the genre because of its futile and nihilistic ending. In a scene that recalls the beginning of *Native Son* (1940), the conclusion of *Blind Man with a Pistol* features a rat that "looked up through murderous red eyes and Coffin Ed shot it through the center of its forehead" (237), while the ghetto erupts in riots. Himes's summarized conclusion seems to convey the reader's own interpretive imbalance: "That don't make any sense" (240).

Those readers coming to his novels expecting racial protest and crypto-Marxist solutions suggestive of Richard Wright's work are also disappointed. *Cotton Comes to Harlem*, for example, parodies the "Back-to-Africa" movement. Marcus Garvey's vision of a black-nationalist movement is not treated seriously; instead, the villain Deke O'Malley, denounced by the novel's living members of the Garveyite movement, simply uses Garvey as a reference to gull sentimental victims. Himes complements the "Back-to-Africa" movement with a "Back-to-the-Southland" movement headed by another absurd con artist, Colonel Robert L. Calhoun, a white-haired and goateed "aristocrat" dressed as a southern plantation owner. Calhoun offers to solve African Americans problems by returning them to the South, playing upon their sentimentality and nostalgia for the lost "Rural Folk." Surely neither "solution" is viable—or even suggested seriously in the novel. As Coffin Ed and Grave Digger walk through a tenement, almost overcome by the smell of urine in the hallways, they muse on their own solution to the degradation and squalor of the poor:

"What American slums need is toilets," Coffin Ed said. Smelling odors of cooking, loving, hair frying, dogs farting, cats pissing, boys masturbating and the stale fumes of stale wine and black tobacco, Grave Digger said, "That wouldn't help much." (51)

In Himes's fictive world, nothing, especially detective work, seems to help much.

What, then, of Chester Himes's artistic achievement as a writer of detective novels? How are we to assess his work? Himes is concerned mainly to revise and reshape the formulae of the detective novel; but surely he does more than this—and to determine precisely what he *does* is to call into question the socio-political nature of reader-response literary analysis, especially since theorists are often indirect or evasive in treating how a (white) reader confronts a text written by an African-American—particularly a political revolutionary like Himes.

Very recently, the reader-reception paradigm has been used effectively in discussing detective fiction as a genre.[2] Briefly, reader-response criticism examines the phenomenological effects of a text on a reader or on "interpretive communities." In essence, the reader in this model is forced to engage with a text to shape its meaning himself/herself; no passive recipient of a predetermined meaning, the reader actively processes a text that is filled with gaps, erasures, and blanks, to construct a meaning that is his/her own. Aesthetic meaning emerges, then, from a process of interaction between the reader and the fissiparous text, though the text "structures" the meanings the reader devises. The aesthetic object, which Wolfgang Iser in *The Act of Reading* identifies as the meaning of the text, varies "in accordance with the social and cultural code of each individual reader" (93).

The "social and cultural code," however, remains problematic. Robert B. Stepto has brilliantly called into question the reader-response approach offered by Iser, Stanley Fish, Jonathan Culler, and other theorists. Although Stepto's theory is far too complex for extensive treatment here, it offers us a way to understand Himes's artistic method. Stepto has proposed that African-American writers, predicting the skepticism or even hostility of their readers, have been led to "create and refine . . . a discourse of distrust" (304). The reader-response model stresses the unreliability of the text and situates the reader alongside the author, continually controlling, rewriting, or assaulting the text. But Stepto contends that an African-American author posits instead an unreliable *reader* who himself/herself must be assaulted:

In Afro-American storytelling texts especially, rhetoric and narrative strategy combine time and again to declare that the principal unreliable factor in the storytelling paradigm is the reader (white American readers, obviously, but blacks as well), and that acts of creative communication are fully initiated not when the text is assaulted but when the reader gets "told"—or "told off"—in such a way that he or she finally begins to *hear*. It is usually in this way that most written tales express their distrust not just of readers but of official literate culture in general. (309)

This is precisely what Himes is accomplishing: He is using the detective genre to "tell us off."

But Himes's ultimate purpose is not merely to vent his spite. Himes's work instead may be described in Roland Barthes's words as the most privileged "writerly" text: "The text that imposes a state of loss, the text that discomforts . . . [and] unsettles the reader's historical, cultural, psychological assumptions, the consistency of his tastes, values, memories, brings to crisis his relation with language" (14). If conventional detective fiction is "discernibly quietistic, politically and socially" (Christianson 146) because it mitigates the anxieties of its readership, Himes does exactly the reverse. He does not ignore literary conventions; he defies them. He structures his work in patterns of violated expectations; he first asks us to read his novels as literature but then deliberately leads us to reject the critical conventions on which our readings are based. Thus, the fictive frame of his work is constantly being broken—involuntarily, the reader of Himes's literature is led to see the actual consequences of racism in America. Describing one of his earlier books, Himes writes, "I had intended to write about the deadly venom of racial prejudice which kills both racists and their victims" (*My Life of Absurdity* 1). By "telling us off" in his detective fiction, Chester Himes keeps alive in the reader's imagination the struggle against oppression, domination, and racism.

NOTES

1. Stephen F. Milliken, *Chester Himes: A Critical Appraisal*; Edward Margolies, *Native Sons: A Critical Study of Twentieth Century Black American Authors*, 87-101; Raymond Nelson, "Domestic Harlem: The Fiction of Chester Himes," 161-76; Robert E. Skinner, *Two Guns from Harlem: The Detective Fiction of Chester Himes*.
2. See esp. Porter, *The Pursuit of Crime*; Peter Hühn, "The Detective as Reader: Narrativity and Reading Concepts in Detective Fiction," 451-66; George N. Dove, "The Detection Formula and the Act of Reading," 25-37.

REFERENCES

Barthes, Roland. *The Pleasure of the Text*, translated by Richard Miller. New York: Hill and Wang, 1975.
Christianson, Scott R. "A Heap of Broken Images: Hardboiled Detective Fiction and the Discourse(s) of Modernity." In *The Cunning Craft*, edited by Ronald Walker and June Frazer, 135-48. Macomb, IL: Yeast, 1990.
Dove, George N. "The Detection Formula and the Act of Reading." In *The Cunning Craft*, edited by Ronald Walker and June Frazer, 25-37. Macomb, IL: Yeast, 1990.
Franklin, H. Bruce. *The Victim as Criminal and Artist: Literature from the American Prison*. New York: Oxford University Press, 1978.
Himes, Chester. *All Shot Up*. New York: Avon, 1960.
____. *Blind Man with a Pistol*. New York: William Morrow, 1969.
____. *Cotton Comes to Harlem*. New York: Random House, 1965, 1988.
____. *The Crazy Kill*. New York: Avon, 1959.
____. *The Heat's On*. New York: Random House, 1966, 1988.
____. *My Life of Absurdity*. New York: Doubleday and Co., 1976.
____. *The Quality of Hurt: The Early Years*. New York: Paragon House, 1971-1972.
____. *A Rage in Harlem* (originally entitled *For Love of Imabelle*). New York: Random House, 1957, 1985.
____. *The Real Cool Killers*. New York: Random House, 1959, 1987.
Hühn, Peter. "The Detective as Reader: Narrativity and Reading Concepts in Detective Fiction." *Modern Fiction Studies* 33, no. 3 (Autumn 1987): 451-66.
Iser, Wolfgang. *The Act of Reading: A Theory of Aesthetic Response*. Baltimore: Johns Hopkins University Press, 1978.
Jameson, Fredric. *The Political Unconscious: Narrative as a Socially Symbolic Act*. Ithaca, NY: Cornell University Press, 1981.

Knight, Stephen. *Form and Ideology in Crime Fiction*. Bloomington: Indiana University Press, 1980.

Margolies, Edward. *Native Sons: A Critical Study of Twentieth Century Black American Authors*. Philadelphia: J. B. Lippincott, 1968.

____. *Which Way Did He Go: The Private Eye in Dashiell Hammett, Raymond Chandler, Chester Himes, and Ross Macdonald*. New York: Holmes and Meier, 1982.

Milliken, Stephen F. *Chester Himes: A Critical Appraisal*. Columbia: University of Missouri Press, 1976.

Muller, Gilbert H. *Chester Himes*. Boston: Twayne, 1989.

Nelson, Raymond. "Domestic Harlem: The Fiction of Chester Himes." *Virginia Quarterly Review* 48, no. 2 (Spring 1972). Reprinted in *Dimensions of Detective Fiction*, edited by Pat Browne et al. 161-76. Bowling Green, OH: Popular Press, 1976.

Porter, Dennis. *The Pursuit of Crime: Art and Ideology in Detective Fiction*. New Haven, CT: Yale University Press, 1981.

Rabinowitz, Peter J. "Chandler Comes to Harlem: Racial Politics in the Thrillers of Chester Himes." In *The Sleuth and the Scholar: Origins, Evolution and Current Trends in Detective Fiction*, edited by Barbara Rader and Howard Zettler. Westport, CT: Greenwood Press, 1988.

Skinner, Robert E. *Two Guns from Harlem: The Detective Fiction of Chester Himes*. Bowling Green, OH: Popular Press, 1989.

Sontag, Susan. *Against Interpretation*. New York: Farrar, Straus and Giroux, 1966.

Stepto, Robert B. "Distrust of the Reader in Afro-American Narratives." In *Reconstructing American Literary History*, edited by Sacvan Bercovitch, 300–322. Cambridge, MA: Harvard University Press, 1986.

Williams, John A. "My Man Himes: An Interview with Chester Himes." In *Flashbacks: A Twenty-Year Diary of Article Writing*. Garden City, NY: Doubleday, 1974.

6

Murdering Traditional Assumptions: The Jewish-American Mystery

Diana Arbin Ben-Merre

In England's Golden Age mysteries "foreigners lead dangerous lives . . . and men otherwise exemplary die for merely ethnic reasons" (Grella 97). Indeed, according to Dilys Winn, "the number of gratuitous insults dangled upon Jews in these books quite exceeds the reprimands, slights and minor indignities suffered on anyone else" (133). Although Winn does not indicate which group was the beneficiary of the most contempt during America's Golden Age, similar xenophobic attitudes towards ethnics prevailed. It was not until the 1960s, with the success of Harry Kemelman's Rabbi Small series, that Jewish figures began to enter the traditional mystery as significant characters.

Today, when more than a dozen writers include Jewish detectives in their novels, it may be difficult to keep in mind the significance of Kemelman's achievement. Rabbi Small's immediate contemporaries, Lesley Egan's Jesse Falkenstein and Richard and Frances Lockridge's Nathan Shapiro, suggest the nature of this achievement. When Kemelman's first novel was published in 1964, there was one Falkenstein novel, *A Case for Appeal* (1961), and several Shapiro novels, beginning with *The Faceless Adversary* (1956). Falkenstein, a lawyer, can display occasional eloquence in defense of his underdog clients: "Justice and injustice my people know something about, and wasn't it truly said, *Behold, it is a stiffnecked people*. So I am, . . . when it comes to forms of justice—and ordinary fair play" (*Avenger* 126-27).[1] More typically, his Judaic heritage is reduced to quotations from biblical commentators and wisdom literature. These quotations often have the effect of identifying tags because they lack a context in which they could be meaningful:

[He thought] of that funny old great-aunt of a second cousin—the cousin who'd married that Irish fellow. Great-aunt straight from the Old Country, not much English, and what she had she used in talking about her illustrious father, a rabbi if you please, a very learned man—otherwise, the incomprehensible Hebrew until you asked in self-defense what she was talking about. (*Appeal* 148)

A great-aunt from the old country who speaks Hebrew rather than Yiddish suggests a more remarkable family heritage than Falkenstein seems to appreciate. More expressive of his inheritance is discomfort with his name: "Take Falkenstein. Sounds better in English—Falconstone" (*Appeal* 93). His name is even more burdensome for his non-Jewish wife, who deals not with the unfairness of anti-Semitism but the unfairness of being mistaken for a Jew: "The man who owns the thirty-five thousand dollar house . . . obviously expected me to talk Yiddish at him and try to walk off with the silver" (*Evidence* 41).

For Nathan Shapiro, a police detective from Brooklyn whose father was a rabbi, the tradition offers a different kind of burden. Shapiro has the perennially sad face of someone laden with the human failings that he is forced to deal with in the course of his work.[2] His sense of himself as a social outsider offers an important reminder of recent history: "'A room for a day or so? . . . My name is Shapiro.' You made it clear from the start. . . . You gave people an out, if they wanted an out. Saved trouble that way. Enough trouble without carrying a lance" (*Blueberry Pie* 125-26). Although the hotel clerk is welcoming, Shapiro never becomes an insider. Throughout his long, successful career, he continues to see himself as inadequate. He has no respect for his intellect, but, in a twist that may be intended to be comic, he considers himself "good" with a gun.

In contrast to these figures for whom Judaism is defined socially in somewhat fixed and emblematic terms, Rabbi Small is defined in terms of a dynamic, living belief. In fact, the kind of character Small is and the kinds of issues Kemelman deals with illuminate the degree to which Small depends upon the postwar Jewish-American novelists of the 1950s and 1960s. These novelists, of whom Bellow, Malamud, and Roth were the best known, created a cultural space in which Jewish issues were given intrinsic interest and value. In terms of popular culture, it is almost possible to say that Kemelman's Rabbi Small does for Jews in America what Chesterton's Father Brown must have done for Catholics in England. Like Father Brown, Rabbi Small is a small, apparently inoffensive man, whose clothes are inevitably rumpled and whose manner is somewhat abstracted. Rabbi Small is clean-shaven and ordinary and no more embodies the persona of the traditional Golden Age Jew who "would wear a black beard even if he were clean-shaven" (Grossvogel 259) than Father Brown embodies Papist designs on England.

As part of his strategy to demythicize the Jew, Kemelman uses the various motifs that worked to keep Jews apart from the society of the traditional mystery—their outsider status, their relationship to business, their "cleverness"—in order to undermine the assumptions upon which these motifs are based. Kemelman retains but reinterprets the status of detective "outsider" for Rabbi Small, who, like Hercule Poirot or Miss Marple, is both of and apart from his society. But Small's society is more problematic than theirs. Although a clean-shaved Conservative rabbi fits more easily into a small New England town than one of Falkenstein's Orthodox forebears, Small has to deal with many of the ambiguities of living in a larger, more complex America, where even a rabbi can be a suspect in a murder investigation.

However, Kemelman's reinterpretation of the detective "outsider" is most fruitfully exploited in Small's relationship to the Jewish community of Barnard's Crossing, Massachusetts. There, because of his commitment to traditional Jewish laws and rabbinic teaching, Small's congregation, a community of businessmen sharing an ethos that probably is best summed up in Dale Carnegie's *How to Win Friends and Influence People*, generally regard him as a disloyal employee. "He's supposed to be our representative, yet would you hire him as a salesman for your company . . . ?" (*Friday* 24).

When the rabbi, for example, tells an engaged couple that they may not serve unkosher food at their synagogue reception and they complain about losing the deposit given to a caterer, the rabbi informs them that their loss was "no worse than the money you've lost on your temple dues the last few years." When they fail to understand his comment, he elaborates: "Because if in the several years you've been here you haven't found out the principles on which our temple operates, I'd say all the money you paid in annual dues was wasted" (*Tuesday* 16). Even the most rudimentary knowledge of Jewish practices cannot be bought. Jewish values are not business values.

Jewish "cleverness" offers another stumbling block: "'A very clever man—a Jew, of course'" is "the backhanded compliment that Jews are in the habit of receiving from anti-Semites" (Grossvogel 261). Not a genetic trait, whatever "cleverness" the rabbi exhibits results from habits of mind inculcated in Torah study. "Our great scholars spent their lives studying the Talmud, not because the exact interpretation of the Law happened to be germane to their problems at the time . . . but because as a mental exercise it had a tremendous fascination for them. It encouraged them to dredge up from their minds all kinds of ideas" (*Friday* 122).

In keeping with the rabbi's methodology, the solutions to the mysteries in the best novels depend upon more than ordinary detection: "You would have seen it, too, if you weren't conditioned to focus first and foremost on the outsider, the stranger" (*Sunday* 181).

The rabbi's understanding of the place of the stranger, the outsider, is, of course, tied to the central Jewish experience: "And if a stranger sojourn with thee in your land, ye shall not do him wrong . . . for ye were strangers in the land of Egypt" (*Sunday* 153). Despite his capacity to use his special knowledge for such practical purposes as catching criminals, Rabbi Small often is in difficulty with his congregation because of his commitment to Torah values in a congregation that believes that "when you hire a rabbi, you're buying spiritual leadership" (*Monday* 15).

These difficulties illuminate the extent to which Rabbi Small shares some of the qualities of the classical Jewish-American hero, especially the estrangement from one's own community. Although ecumenical significances abound, Small's close friendship with Hugh Lanigan, the Catholic chief of police, also serves to emphasize his isolation from his own community. Rabbi Small's uncertain authority may reflect not only the place of Judaism but, perhaps, also the place of most traditional Western religions in present-day America in their failure to be a center around which a community can sustain itself and flourish. This is particularly significant because Judaism cannot be practiced in the absence of community. Without the sense of community—a community whose injunction is "to be holy, to be a nation of priests, to be a light unto the nation [sic]" (*Tuesday* 141)—Judaism is merely another kind of specialized knowledge or, as one citizen of Barnard's Crossing indicates, a set of odd practices: "Everybody knows they got to cut off your whatsis to make you a Jew" (*Friday* 135).

This discussion suggests the extent to which Small is characterized almost completely in terms of his Jewish beliefs and, as such, is a genuinely new figure in detective fiction.[3] The detectives who follow Kemelman are defined in more secular terms. These characters can be divided into two groups, according to how they deal with the question of Jewish identity. The first group includes those for whom Judaism is part of their identities, apart from particular issues of beliefs or practices. Kathryn Lasky Knight's Calista Jacobs could be their spokesperson: "I was born a Jew. I practice it in my own way. But I am one of those people who has never been very comfortable with anything organized, especially religion" (332). Kinky Friedman's Kinky Friedman and Arthur Lyons' Jacob Asch also belong to this group.[4]

For the second group, Judaism is more problematic and, therefore, more difficult to define. This group includes Charlotte MacLeod's Max Bittersohn, Julie Smith's Rebecca Schwartz, Marissa Piesman's Nina Fischman, James Yaffe's Mom, and Faye Kellerman's Peter Decker.

Because many of the values and beliefs of Judaism do not appear to be very different from those of other religions, being Jewish can be seen as "more a matter of belonging to the Jewish people, the family, than of accepting certain specific beliefs" (*Tuesday* 229). In English literature, destroying the family unit as a way of destroying the Jewish people has a long history that extends from Shylock's daughter Jessica, who stole her father's money and ran off with the Christian Lorenzo, to Dorothy Sayers' Rachel Levy, whose father, Lord Levy, an inconvenient ethnic, tries to prevent her marriage to the Christian Freddy Arbuthnot.

The American novelist Charlotte MacLeod seems more tactful than most as she goes about reconstituting the Jewish family unit. In her Max Bittersohn—Sarah Kelling mysteries, MacLeod equates Judaism with snobbery. The Jewish discomfort with intermarriage is seen as a counterpart to the snobbishness of the moribund New England Kellings, so that, in Bittersohn's marriage to Kelling, both are seen as escaping from a kind of exclusiveness. Because Bittersohn's Judaism is defined by his use of Yiddish pet names for Sarah and by his conviction that dealing with his mother is infinitely more difficult than catching a murderer ("The final battle is yet to come. I'm taking you to meet my mother" [206]), MacLeod may not be wrong in her assessment of Max's Judaism.[5]

Without a specific communal context, Jewish values can be seen as part of a modern tradition of liberalism and social activism. Both Julie Smith's Rebecca Schwartz and Marissa Piesman's Nina Fischman are professional Jewish women whose legal work offers them opportunities for detection. Rebecca Schwartz, like her mother, has only a liberal tradition for support:

"Your father and I have never felt he was good enough for our Rebecca. . . ." "Mom, just because he's only half-Jewish is no reason to condemn him." . . . "Rebecca, how can you hurt me like that! After the way you've been raised, how could you think a thing like that could possibly enter into my feelings?" (108)

Rebecca's attractiveness increases as Smith distances her from both mother and boyfriend. The portrait that then emerges is that of a woman who is a secular Jew. Judaism is part of her identity, but it makes no profound claims on her sense of self.[6]

Marissa Piesman's Nina Fischman is also the product of a liberal secular tradition that seems to have more substance than that of Rebecca Schwartz. However, she too is troubled by some aspects of Orthodox Judaism that her mother apparently discarded with her own parents' taste in furniture: "To Ida, brocade couches meant Orthodox Judaism and all that went with it—narrow mindedness, repression of women and capitalism. Teak was the wood of enlightenment" (56-57). As this passage suggests, the mother is an attractive character, and the relationship between mother and daughter is extremely appealing, almost offering a feminist rebuttal to Roth's *Portnoy's Complaint*.

Despite Piesman's efforts, the logic of popular culture seems to decree that the "real" Jewish mother cannot be moribund for very long. James Yaffe's Mom, a cross between Mrs. Portnoy and Miss Marple—"It's exactly like the Birnbaums that lived upstairs from us in the Bronx" (*Maker* 50)—solves cases for her son, a former New York City policeman, who works as an investigator for the public defender's office in the small western town of Mesa Grande. Despite some rather nice social satire, Mom is too knowing and, naturally, too manipulative. Her son, who has to miss some fairly obvious clues in order to provide Mom with her opportunities, is often made to feel like a fish out of water: "That wasn't unusual for Mom, dangling a tidbit under my nose and then pulling it away just as I was about to snap at it" (*Maker* 91-92).[7] In this context, Jews are people from New York who do not celebrate Christmas, and the virtues of Judaism are such that even a rabbi can be a *mensch*, but God seems to be on the other side: "And the mountains, when you glimpsed them from the ends of the cross streets, looked like white-haired giants. Patriarchs from some old-fashioned illustrated edition of the Bible. On a day like this, it wasn't quite as hard as usual to understand why the people in this area are so obsessed with God" (*Murder* 106).

Whether this treatment of Judaism stems from the discomfort that many Americans feel with cultural differences or from difficulties with certain aspects of Jewish life, these novels dismiss the possibility that Judaism as a religion may have something valuable to offer. Significantly, none of these novels presents characters who are part of a viable Jewish community.

This community is present in *The Ritual Bath*, Faye Kellerman's first novel (published in 1986), which is set in an isolated Orthodox Jewish community. It is ironic that the Golden Age mystery, which excluded Jews from serious concern, is the vehicle for this extremely successful mystery. This form, which depicts an isolated edenic community whose existence is threatened by violence from within (Auden 17, 19), is an excellent vehicle for the portrayal of Jewish values. These exist most fully in a communal context.

The theme of community is particularly important because this mystery deals with the ways individuals can bind themselves to a society with which they can share a history and traditions. In helping Peter Decker, her detective, to begin to establish his connections to Judaism, Kellerman employs what might be described as the Daniel Deronda principle. George Eliot's Daniel Deronda, as we may recall, was brought up to be a Christian gentleman. When he gives up this heritage for Judaism, he is portrayed as discovering his Jewish roots rather than rejecting his Christian upbringing. Like Deronda, Kellerman's Peter Decker was brought up by Christians. A more modern, clearly American figure, Decker is given the aristocratic tokens of a ranch and horses rather than Eton or Cambridge. He has been aware of his Jewish parentage, but, until his meeting with the beautiful Rina Lazarus, a young, observant Jewish widow, he has not attempted to find a way of embodying this heritage in his life. Here the Daniel Deronda principle is particularly useful because Decker's desire to return to his origins becomes more than a strategy to deflect criticism—it becomes a way of making his quest to understand his religious origins less a special Jewish quest than an existential one.[8]

With the universalizing of Peter's quest, the differences between Kellerman's goals and Kemelman's goals become evident. Kemelman, while insisting on the differences between Jews and others, was animated by the need to dispel negative stereotypes. Kellerman is interested in suggesting that the differences between Jews and others are illusory. Here the nature of the characters Kellerman has chosen becomes important. While they share a commitment to their religious community, neither Lazarus nor Decker represents its norms. Without the religious context, Decker and Lazarus are familiar figures: Decker, the tough cop with a special past; Lazarus, the beautiful woman who, for some reason, is unavailable. It is to Kellerman's credit, however, that by insisting upon the seriousness of their religious concerns, she is able to address important religious issues.

Appearing almost twenty years after the first Rabbi Small novel, *The Ritual Bath* provides a way of measuring how un–self-conscious the Jewish mystery has become. Here the Edenic community is a society of black-bearded Jews—an enclosed orthodox Jewish community that is organized around a yeshivah, an academy of Jewish learning. When one of the chief suspects, who is of the community and embodies its values, helps to fell the villain with the classical Jewish weapon, a heavy talmudic tome, his courage and suffering are acknowledged in a witty and appropriate reinterpretation of the final Golden Age gathering. This takes place not "around a table in the library, at a pub, a dinner party" but in the manner of a Hasidic dance in the woods, an event that, like the other gatherings, serves to affirm the values of the community and the fact that it has been "recreated anew from the shambles of a temporary disorder" (Grella 99).

The success of *The Ritual Bath* must have created difficulties for Kellerman. Because a yeshivah community is truly closed, it offers fewer opportunities for mystery than a place like Chipping Cleghorn or St. Mary Mead. Perhaps the most telling example, however, is offered by Faye Kellerman's second novel, *Sacred and Profane*, which apparently intends to contrast Decker's love for Lazarus with the kind of violence that offers a parody of this in pornographic films. However, the crime that is the focus of the novel takes place so far from the Jewish community that its values seem private and irrelevant. Therefore, the real issue becomes not Judaism itself, but the very possibility of religious belief: "Lately the crap was beginning to get to him. The dichotomy—one minute he was a spiritual being, praying, seeking a higher order in his life; the next, knee deep in scum and shit. He was living in two worlds, not sure which part of his life was real and which was an undercover assignment" (184).

Decker has to learn that although the world of Jewish observance, a world of "rules" and "rituals," may seem to be apart from "the real world" where "there's no blacks and white [sic]—only goddam muddy grays" (221), this world, too, contains ambiguities. When Decker complains that he can experience a sense of God's presence and then feel the same absolute sense of His absence, he is told by Rabbi Schulman, whose faith has survived Auschwitz and the destruction of his family, that uncertainty is a condition of belief (236).

Just as there are moments of clarity with regard to God's presence, so too there are moments of transcendent clarity in the "real" gray world. In one such moment, Decker "suddenly" feels "the enormity of playing judge, jury, and executioner" (324) and refuses to play those roles. The novel ends with Decker, more in touch with himself than before, facing "east, peering into the advancing dimness. Feeling at peace, he took out a siddur and said his evening prayers" (329). Although his prayer is specifically Jewish, the feelings evoked by the passage are universal.

Kellerman's subsequent novels, *Milk and Honey* and *Day of Atonement*, also have the double plots that suggest the continuing difficulties of integrating Decker's public life as a detective with his private life as a *ba'al teshuvah*, a returning Jew. Clearly these double plots also are intended to suggest the difficulties of trying to integrate the world of secular endeavors with the world of religious belief.

The first plot of *Milk and Honey* deals with Decker the detective, who finds an abandoned child and investigates four murders; the second with Decker the friend, who unofficially investigates charges that his buddy Abel slashed a prostitute. Although the second mystery seems less complex than the first, it proves more difficult because it questions the very possibility of moral action. Abel's name suggests the issues Kellerman begins to deal with, but it does not quite prepare for the ironies: Decker had the moral will to act as his "brother's keeper," but he could not have known or—even with knowledge—been able to control the results of his actions. "'What was Peter's crime?'. . . 'Saving my life,' Abel said" (329).

This second plot underlines the fact that no act is simple or self-contained. Even Decker's mentor Rabbi Schulman, who tells how, as a young man, he killed a young Nazi soldier "for my sake and the sake of . . . the Jewish people," wakes up from dreams "about that boy" and asks himself: "If I was so right, why does God allow me to see this child's terror as clearly as the day I shot him?" (347).[9] Kellerman's insistence on moral ambiguity places Decker in a context where he seems to be a more modern figure than Rabbi Small, a traditional detective whose mysteries are self-contained.

The first story in *Milk and Honey*—the abandoned child and the four murders —while complex, seems to invoke traditional methods of detection, the working out of motives and timetables, the correct reading of signs. Even though the correct interpretation of clues is obviously necessary to free Abel, the value of the second story rests in the questions that it raises about the nature of moral action. If we read the first plot in the terms in which we have learned to read the second, we realize it is only Peter's emotional distance from this mystery that makes it appear that the issues were completely resolved.

People using other people. Decker tried to muster up some indignation, but his self-righteousness felt hollow and flat.

   And in the background all Decker heard was the pathetic cry of [a bereaved lover calling for his beloved] *Linda, Linda, Linda.* (368)

It is the presence of the second plot, which makes Decker's investigation a quest "not for a specific criminal, but for a *raison d'etre*, a meaning in character and relationship" (Chandler, 57). When the second plot redefines the search in a theological context ("Why does God allow me to see this child's terror?"), it raises questions about the nature of human action and understanding. These questions receive further exploration in *Day of Atonement*, Kellerman's fourth Decker-Lazarus mystery.

This mystery also develops a theme that Kellerman began to examine in her characterization of the closed, inbred Darcys, the farming family of the first plot of *Milk and Honey*. The biblical overtones of the title and the patriarchal order of the Darcy clan seem intended to raise questions about the nature of closed societies. Unlike the closed Yeshivah community, whose organization is determined by Jewish law and custom, the Darcys form a false community that has no substance apart from the will of the patriarch. However, the weight and cohesion Kellerman initially assigned to a traditional Jewish community in her first novel, *The Ritual Bath*, is also questioned in *Day of Atonement*.

The Ritual Bath was set in a California yeshivah and contained a single plot—meeting and protecting Lazarus was part of the way Decker solved the mystery and also began to come to terms with some aspects of his identity. The return to an orthodox community in the Brooklyn setting of *Day of Atonement*, far from signaling unity, measures their separation from their original world. Here, the first plot concerns an endangered runaway orthodox boy; the second, the Decker-Lazarus marriage and Decker's discoveries about his past. Worldly concerns seem to triumph when the second is resolved as both Decker and Lazarus agree to undergo therapy for the "horrendous stresses that need to be dealt with" (346). But the first plot shows how one person becomes a victim, another a victimizer, and how both these categories begin to overlap. Even after the criminals are found and guilt is portioned out, the final image is that of a victim who is also a victimizer praying to a God who does not answer.

This image almost can be said to symbolize the predicament of Kellerman's characters. To understand their situation, it is useful to recall one of the main assumptions of Kemelman's Rabbi Small series, written almost twenty years earlier. In Rabbi Small's world, Judaism was presented as one of several possible Western religions. There are references to Episcopalians, for example, because Small's congregants find the Episcopalian minister's bearing so much more dignified and appropriate than their rabbi's. Catholicism is presented as the main "other" religion in the community perhaps because, like Jews, Catholics also are outsiders in small prerevolutionary New England towns. Therefore, despite the difficulties Rabbi Small has with his congregation, Kemelman's novels assume that an individual lives in a world where some kind of religious affiliation is the norm. This sense is so strong that when Rabbi Small is threatened with the loss of his position in the synagogue, he is able to assert that he still is the rabbi of all the Jews in Barnard's Crossing. This sense of religious identification is lost in Faye Kellerman's novels, where religion is so absent from daily life that the only religious community we see is the closed world of the yeshivah. And the yeshivah replicates a European way of life established centuries ago.

How can Decker, who is so American that he owns a ranch, connect its values with those of this closed community that represents his heritage? And how can he connect both with his life as a detective in a world of often unspeakable crimes? And here, in Decker's world, where religion is so absent from daily life, Judaism can be seen as a symbol for the reasoned and difficult act of religious commitment in a world that does not even experience nostalgia for what has been lost. The differences between Kemelman's and Kellerman's novels cannot be understood by the almost twenty-year gap between them; these novels dramatize the differences between a world where religious affiliation is seen as a "natural" part of an individual's identity and a world where religious affiliation—of any kind—is presented as an act of existential faith.

Despite the differences between the worlds that they create, both Kemelman and Kellerman, like many other writers of Jewish-American mysteries, helped to demystify the Jewish character. In so doing, they created an environment in which black-bearded Jews—or any Jews—no longer are viewed in the context of traditional stereotypes. Once Jews are seen as subjects rather than objects, they no longer appear inordinately materialistic or overly clever. Like their non-Jewish counterparts, Jews often inhabit a world where the experience of God's absence can sometimes be more compelling than the experience of His presence, a world in which everyone can be an outsider.

The contributions of these writers of the Jewish-American mystery novel have helped to make the Jewish experience universal and therefore comprehensible. Certainly, the many writers and the great variety of sleuths suggest the release of energy from an audience that no longer has to hold its collective breath, wondering whether the next page will contain not a body but bland assumptions about names or noses.

Still, ambiguities remain. Rabbi Small's clean-shaven suburban style and his close friendship with Hugh Lanigan may be reassuring for the wrong reasons. Kellerman's black-bearded Jews, whose religious concerns are universal, may offer similar reassurances. Both suggest that to be acceptable, the outsider has to be recast in terms that the dominant culture can understand and accept.

NOTES

1. Although his language is eloquent, his choice of words is odd because "stiffnecked" was the term God used to berate the Jewish people when they refused to turn to Him.

2. Here Jewishness is used as a quick way of characterizing an individual with moral concerns. Although Donald Westlake's Levine is a more complex character than Shapiro, Westlake's use of Judaism in *Levine* is somewhat similar. In his introduction to this collection, Westlake suggests that Levine represents aspects of personality that normally are submerged. Therefore, as a character, Levine probably has more affinities with John Updike's Beck (also a Jew) than with Shapiro.

The exalted goodness of these figures may be behind Irving Weinman's Lenny Schwartz, another New York City policeman. Schwartz, whose connections to Judaism are more tenuous than Shapiro's, once took a bribe from a drug dealer. With this as background, Weinman seems concerned to discover how Schwartz can reinvent himself as a moral man and perhaps also as a Jew.

3. Small was such a new figure that, according to prefatory material in an early paperback edition of *Friday the Rabbi Slept Late* (cited below), the original publishers received orders for such texts as *Friday, the Rabbit Slept Late* and *Freddy, the Rabbit Slept Late*.

Small also may be the only fictional detective cleric who is given the opportunity to speak about religious belief and practices in a special text. Although *Conversations with Rabbi Small* has the format of a novel, its purpose, as the cover copy proclaims, is to "[explore] a greater mystery: The meaning of Judaism."

Joseph Telushkin's Rabbi Daniel Winter, a younger, more troubled version of Rabbi David Small, is a somewhat more modern character. He is the host of a radio talk show, and he can cook a sabbath dinner. However, he shares many of Small's qualities, especially his moral stubbornness, and the inevitable difficulties with his congregation. Especially interesting is *An Eye for an Eye*, where Telushkin deals powerfully with the gap between what he sees as "Judaism's priorities and those of American criminal law" (257).

4. Kinky Friedman's detective of the same name says "I located an old Italian salami that had fallen into the back of the refrigerator and had been there since about Purim of 1974" (*Greenwich* 109). "Purim" indicates some Jewish connection, "Italian salami" a non-Jewish style of eating, and the general tone a degree of ease with both.

Jacob Asch tosses off similar Jewish references without much expectation that they will be understood. When invited, for example, "to get dressed and come with us, please? District Attorney Carew would like to talk to you," Asch responds, "Not until Soviet Jewry is freed," a phrase that, in 1977, must have signified "never" (*Ringer* 66). Asch sees himself as "an agnostic half-Jew" (*Floor* 75), "the product of a mixed marriage—a Jewish father and an Episcopalian mother." He feels "a strong cultural bond to Judaism, but the faith part of it had never really taken hold."

His Jewish connection depends, in part, on the Holocaust: "Maybe I was just plugged into some common pool of paranoia . . . engendered by the number six million." Because of the Holocaust, only a sadistic God is possible: "And I'd come to the conclusion years ago that if there was a God up there watching over us, he had to be dressed in black leather" (*Floor* 10-11).

For Kinky Friedman, whose patron saints are Hank Williams, Anne Frank, and Ernie Kovacs (*Lone Star* 51), the Holocaust also is central to his identification with Judaism: "I was too young to have been there at the time, but I was a Jew. There would always be a little piece of yesterday in my eye" (*Flyer* 186).

5. See *The Bilbao Looking Glass*. Despite this Kelling is shown trying to reconcile her Christmas expectations with "what might be acceptable to her recently acquired Jewish in-laws" ("Cozy" 4).

6. See, for example, Smith's *Dead in the Water*. A liberal political ethos also seems sufficient for Roger L. Simon's private detective Moses Wine.

7. Whether the Jewish mother is portrayed as overly intrusive or merely indifferent, she never seems adequate. The mother of Canadian writer Howard Engel's detective Benny Cooperman is used to provide an index of how *noir* his world really is: "I hope you've had your lunch, Benny. Your father hasn't been to the store yet. I'm down to two eggs and I've had them since April" (28).

8. Here it is interesting to consider the English writer S. T. Haymon's Benjamin Jurnet. Although her Detective-Inspector is learning about Judaism because his beloved Miriam promised to marry him if he became a Jew, a reference to "Jurnet of Angleby, the Rothschild of the Middle Ages," suggests that Haymon also may be considering the Deronda principle (24).

9. The language of the passage, which first describes the Nazi soldier as a young man, then as a boy, and then as a child, seems to recapitulate a fairly complex process of moral development. A young man at the time of the murder, Schulman first describes the Nazi similarly—"a young man—around eighteen, nineteen." In life, he was a degraded figure "dressed in a dirty uniform . . . roaming about half-dazed, his eyes glazed over." But his real degradation is moral: When he saw Schulman, he "snarled, and fired

out one word . . . *Juden.*" Not this image, but the final dream image of the child's terror yields moral meaning. Schulman believes that God allows him to see "this child's terror" because He wanted him "to experience the fragility of life. As that boy's life was in my hands, so I am in [His] hands" (347-48).

REFERENCES

Auden, W. H. "The Guilty Vicarage." In *Detective Fiction*, edited by Robin W. Winks. Rev. ed. Woodstock, VT: Countryman Press, 1988.

Chandler, Raymond. *Raymond Chandler Speaking*, edited by Dorothy Gardiner and Katherine Sorley Walker. New York: Houghton Mifflin, 1962. Reprint. Freeport, NY: Books for Libraries, 1971.

Egan, Lesley [Elizabeth Linington]. *Against the Evidence*. New York: Harper, 1962.

____. *A Case for Appeal*. New York: Harper, 1961.

____. *Some Avenger, Rise!* New York: Harper, 1966. Reprint. Popular Library, n.d.

Engel, Howard. *A City Called July*. New York: St. Martin's Press, 1986.

Friedman, Kinky. *A Case of Lone Star*. New York: William Morrow, 1987. Reprint. New York: Berkley, 1988.

____. *Frequent Flyer*. New York: William Morrow, 1989. Reprint. New York: Berkley, 1990.

____. *Greenwich Killing Time*. New York: William Morrow, 1986. Reprint. New York: Berkley, 1987.

Grella, George. "The Formal Detective Novel." In *Detective Fiction*, edited by Robin W. Winks. Rev. ed. Woodstock, VT: Countryman Press, 1988.

Grossvogel, David I. "Agatha Christie: Containment of the Unknown." In *The Poetics of Murder*, edited by Glenn W. Most and William W. Stowe. San Diego: Harcourt Brace, 1983.

Haymon, S. T. *Ritual Murder*. New York: St. Martin's Press, 1982.

Kellerman, Faye. *Day of Atonement*. New York: William Morrow, 1991.

____. *Milk and Honey*. New York: William Morrow, 1990. Reprint. New York: Ballantine, 1991.

____. *The Ritual Bath*. New York: Arbor House, 1986. Reprint. New York: Ballantine, 1987.

____. *Sacred and Profane*. New York: Arbor House, 1987. Reprint. New York: Ballantine, 1988.

Kemelman, Harry. *Conversations with Rabbi Small*. New York: William Morrow, 1981.

____. *Friday the Rabbi Slept Late*. New York: Crown, 1964. Reprint. New York: Fawcett, 1965.

____. *Monday the Rabbi Took Off*. New York: G. P. Putnam's 1972. Reprint. New York: Fawcett, 1973.

____. *Sunday the Rabbi Stayed Home*. New York: G. P. Putnam's, 1969. Reprint. New York: Fawcett, 1970.

____. *Tuesday the Rabbi Saw Red*. New York: Arthur Fields, 1973. Reprint. New York: Fawcett, 1975.

Knight, Kathryn Lasky. *Mortal Wounds*. New York: Summit, 1990. Reprint. New York: Pocket, 1991.

Lockridge, Richard and Frances. *Murder and Blueberry Pie*. Philadelphia: J. B. Lippincott, 1959.

Lyons, Arthur. *Dead Ringer*. New York: Mason/Charter, 1977. Reprint. New York: Holt, 1983.

____. *The Killing Floor*. New York: Mason/Charter, 1976. Reprint. New York: Holt, 1982.

MacLeod, Charlotte. *The Bilbao Looking Glass*. New York: Doubleday, 1983. Reprint. New York: Avon, 1984.

____. "A Cozy for Christmas." In *Mistletoe Mysteries*. New York: Mysterious Press, 1989.

Piesman, Marissa. *Unorthodox Practices*. New York: Pocket, 1989.

Smith, Julie. *The Sourdough Wars*. New York: Walker, 1984.

Telushkin, Joseph. *An Eye for an Eye*. New York: Doubleday, 1991.

Westlake, Donald. *Levine*. New York: Tom Doherty Associates, 1985.

Winn, Dilys. *Murder Ink*. Rev. ed. New York: Workman, 1984.

Yaffe, James. *Mom Meets Her Maker*. New York: St. Martin's Press, 1990. Reprint. Toronto: Worldwide, 1991.

____. *A Nice Murder for Mom*. New York: St. Martin's Press, 1988. Reprint. Toronto: Worldwide, 1990.

7

Gender (De)Mystified: Resistance and Recuperation in Hard-Boiled Female Detective Fiction

Timothy Shuker-Haines and Martha M. Umphrey

What should we make of the recent emergence of the female hard-boiled detective? In a literary-historical sense she is an oxymoron, standing outside the gendered traditions of both the classic female detective and the tough-guy dick. The classic archetype, a Miss Marple or a Jessica Fletcher, generally operates within the domestic sphere, solving drawing-room crimes and reestablishing harmony through a combination of skillful listening, good sense, and intuitive judgment about character.[1] She uses her social knowledge and skills to identify the criminal and thus locate the source of social disruption, purifying and restabilizing society. The hard-boiled detective stands in stark opposition to this female figure. His locale is not the drawing room but the liminal zone of the criminal underworld, and his qualities are not intuition and social knowledge but violence and a personal code of honor. Whereas the classic detective novel presents a stable social order with an isolated crime, hard-boiled fiction presents a world filled with corruption, destabilized by the dangerous allure of female sexuality. With his strict code of honor and renunciation, the hard-boiled hero embodies a vision of righteousness and justice.[2]

The hard-boiled detective would thus appear to be a necessarily male figure, defined by his emphasis on violence, individuation, and horror of female sexuality. David Glover (1989) has argued that the hard-boiled tradition was developed as a masculine reclaiming of the detective novel, which was seen as overly feminized, dominated by detectives who were female (Miss Marple, Harriet Vane) or insufficiently masculine (Hercule Poirot, Peter Wimsey). Thus, the gender confusion inherent in the female hard-boiled detective has the potential to destabilize radically this gendered opposition between classic and hard-boiled detective fiction by problematizing both the construction of the detective and the socially restorative function of detection.

Yet these potentials are not consistently realized when the detective's sex is changed, as a comparison of Sue Grafton's *F Is for Fugitive* and Sara Paretsky's *Blood Shot* reveals. Each novel foregrounds gender as central to both the construction of the detective and the development of the narrative. Yet each writer uses gender differently. Grafton's Kinsey Millhone undermines the relation between gender and biological sex, emphasizing gender's performative nature, but she does so by leaving intact masculinity and feminity—and their hierarchical relation. Paretsky's V. I. Warshawski, on the other hand, presents a valorized female self that enables her to reject both traditional feminine and masculine positions and to offer a critique of male power formations from a feminist perspective, opening up the utopian possibility of community without gender hierarchy. Yet this very utopian vision is based on an uncritical acceptance of the concept of a unified "woman's" identity and community.

Gender relates to the figure of the female hard-boiled detective in complicated and contradictory ways. Initially, both Millhone and Warshawski identify themselves as autonomous and ungendered, and their names reflect this identity metonymically. "Kinsey," Millhone's mother's last name, is ambiguous in gender. "V. I.," on the other hand, stands for "Victoria Iphigenia," an explicitly feminized name that echoes V. I.'s Italian mother's side; yet V. I. rejects that name, allowing her friends to call her, if anything, "Vic." In contrast, hostile acquaintants who want her to circumscribe her activities and behave more like a proper woman (for example, Sergeant Mallory, an old family friend) call her "Vicki." Both "Kinsey" and "Vic" thus operate as ungendered and single-word identifiers that circulate as de facto masculine signifiers in a tough world off-limits to femininity.

At the same time, though, both Millhone and Warshawski identify themselves relationally, either positively or negatively, in a way that accords more with "the feminine" as socially defined.[3] Millhone describes herself in the opening pages of *F Is for Fugitive* as "thirty-two years old, twice married, no kids, currently unattached and likely to remain so given my disposition, which is cautious at best" (FF 3).[4] This description both assumes the primacy of the relational (the male hard-boiled dick could omit his marital status because his bachelorhood would be taken for granted) and rejects it so as to emphasize autonomy.

Warshawski opens her narrative with memories—memories of her childhood in South Chicago and of the people who lived next door while she grew up, the mother-daughter family of Djiaks. Throughout the book she thinks of herself in terms of this former context, especially as it evokes memories of her mother, Gabriella, who once defended the unmarried and pregnant Louisa Djiak from the righteous wrath of her neighbors. Thus, while not explicitly gendering herself, Warshawski is gendered feminine twice over: once as she is constituted in relation to others rather than as contextless and unbound, and again as she reads her identity through the lens of a female community.

In other words, both Millhone and Warshawski remain inscribed to some extent within categories of masculinity and femininity as they are socially constructed. Yet, the strategies mobilized by each to grapple with this gendering differ: Millhone operates independently and remains within a binary heterosexual economy, oscillating between masculine and feminine subject positions; Warshawski uses a mediating, homosocial network of female friends and family to redefine the paradigm of "femininity" via an implicit feminist critique. And just as Warshawski ruptures the heterosexual binary that Millhone caricatures but leaves intact, *Blood Shot* challenges the socially reconstitutive role of detective fiction that *F Is for Fugitive* ultimately accepts.

Kinsey Millhone's persona is gendered substantially as masculine. A woman who has few friends and lives for her work, she is self-consciously, almost parodically male-defined, as, for example, when she describes her tendency to amuse herself with the abridged California Penal code and textbooks on auto theft (FF, 209) rather than engaging in the teatime gossip of a Miss Marple. This masculine stylization and thus her identification with male hard-boiled dicks are perhaps clearest in relation to her gun: "I sat at the kitchen table, loaded seven cartridges in the clip and smacked it home. This was my new handgun. A Davis .32 chrome and walnut with a five-and-a-quarter inch barrel. . . . This one weighed a tidy twenty-two ounces and already felt like an old friend" (FF 149). The gun, described here in such loving detail, becomes a fetishized "old friend" with clear phallic overtones. Millhone's strong identification with her male precursors is further reinforced in this scene by the setting—vapor streetlights filtering through the window, the neon vacancy sign sputtering red light into the room—which has become associated with the hard-boiled tradition through film noir's visual conventions (Place and Peterson 1976; Schrader 1986; Hirsch 1981).

Yet, crucial to Millhone's construction is the psychological mutability of gender, its discontinuity and oscillation. "There was something enormously appealing," she remarks early in the book, "in the idea of setting one persona aside and constructing a second to take its place" (FF 19). She ably plays the feminine role when appropriate, particularly in the context of the heterosexual romance. When she and Dwight Shales, a potential suspect, have dinner for example, they discuss their leisure activities (his is backpacking, hers the penal code); but as the scene grows more intimate she quickly shifts gears: "I listened with both eyes and one ear trying to discern what was really going on. . . . While his mouth made noises . . . his eyes said something else. I disconnected my brain and fine-tuned my receiver, picking up his code. This man was emotionally available" (FF 209). Most notable about this passage is the extremity of the gender switch: She disconnects the "male" logic of her brain so as to engage her "female" sexual intuition; she moves from the penal code to sexual dalliance.[5] Thus, even as she refuses the biological "naturalness" of gender identity in this oscillation, she remains caught within a heterosexual economy that posits two distinct genders (so distinct as to be parodic), unwilling to escape or reimagine the gender roles that define them.

Just as Millhone's character is grounded in the heterosexual binary, so too is the narrative of *F Is for Fugitive*, which centers on the psychic dramas of two groups: Daughters yearning for paternal love and patriarchs succumbing to the temptations of illicit sex. Millhone is called into a small town to investigate the murder of Jean Timberlake, the promiscuous, illegitimate daughter of Shana Timberlake, "the town roundheel." The town's leading citizens (men, of course) come under suspicion as Millhone discovers that each was sexually involved with either Jean or Shana. Doctor Dunne, the town physician, turns out to have been Jean's father. Reverend Haws, the minister at the town's only church, had sex with Jean every week in his office before choir practice. Shales, the high school principal, had gotten Jean pregnant just before her death. With the pillars of society thus implicated in a young girl's demise, the way is open for a critique of the sexual oppression and abuse of women.

Yet, rather than condemning the men's behavior, Millhone forgives it. All these men had wives with failing bodies or minds—Mrs. Dunne had paranoid schizophrenia; Mrs. Shales, multiple sclerosis; Mrs. Haws, a serious skin condition. Millhone views these women as do their husbands—with pity, contempt, and revulsion. By pathologizing the female body, Millhone identifies with and forgives the men driven by such extreme circumstances to extramarital sex.

Male innocence is further reinforced by the overwhelming power of female promiscuity and sexual aggression. Millhone describes Shana, for example, as "exhibitionistic" when she dances in the local bar and notes how Shana has "no modesty at all" (FF 128). Jean is seen as the instigator in her affairs with both Haws and Shales and is described as "insatiable," driven by "a need to dominate." "We were at her mercy," one of her high school paramours says, "because we wanted her so much" (FF 118). This focus on Jean's sexual power leads to the extraordinary implication that a high school principal's sexual affair with a student is a function not of his power, but of hers. There is no correlation between the social power of the men involved and their sexual activities; in the face of the dangerous and disruptive sexuality of Shana and Jean, they are helpless.

Here we find ourselves back in the traditional dynamics of the detective novel; female sexuality is a disruptive force that threatens the social order and must be punished.[6] This is hard-boiled with a twist, for at least the traditional femmes fatales—Brigid O'Shaughnessy in *The Maltese Falcon*, Phyllis Dietrichson in *Double Indemnity*—offered a thrilling vision of transforming their sexual charisma into material and personal power. Shana and Jean Timberlake, on the other hand, remain merely disruptive, reaping no such benefits.

This patriarchal vision of female desire as dangerous ties the revelations of social scandal to the family romance at the heart of the narrative. Millhone, originally hired by Royce Fowler to free his son Bailey, discovers that the murderer was neither Bailey nor any of the men sexually involved with Jean, but Ann Fowler, Bailey's sister. Ann, obsessively in love with Shales, kills Jean to prevent her pregnancy from ruining him and kills Shana because she believes, incorrectly, that Shana is involved with him.

Thus, the murders of the sexually dangerous women are tied not to men protecting their social standing, but to a jealous woman. The incestuous nature of Ann's jealousy is revealed by her third murder: that of her own mother. Deprived of the love of her stern father, who is interested only in his son Bailey, she both frames Bailey and kills her mother to claim her father's love. It thus becomes clear that Ann's desire for Shales was tied to his paternal function; he was the principal at the school where she was a counselor. Just as Shales's affair with his young student Jean had incestuous overtones, Ann's murder of Jean is meant to open a space she can occupy as the beloved of Shales, the father substitute.

Ultimately, the daughter's yearning for the father implicates Millhone, evoking memories of her sense of loss at the death of her own father when she was five. In the end, Millhone muses on her links with both Jean (who, before she died, was searching for her father) and Ann: "None of us had survived the wounds our fathers inflicted all those years ago. Did he love us? How would we ever know? He was gone and he'd never again be what he was to us in all his haunting perfection" (FF 306).

Yet, the book implies that women can, through self-denial, win a shred of this paternal love. When Ann shoots off her foot after struggling with her father over a gun, she cries, "You were never there for me. . . . You were never there" (FF 305); but at that moment she ends up in his arms. Both shooting off her foot and giving up the gun act as symbolic castrations; Ann relinquishes her claims to phallic power by handing the gun over to her father, and she cripples herself as a form of punishment. Rendered helpless and dependent, she finally gains the paternal embrace. Millhone takes this lesson to heart. While the book opens with Millhone's complaints that her elderly landlord, Henry Pitts, is too doting and threatens her independence, it closes with her determination to treasure him. "He may," she says, "be the closest thing to a father I'll ever have" (FF 307).

The book locates the source of disruption in the daughter's unreciprocated love for the father. The danger of incest, its threat to the patriarchal order, lies in the desires of the daughter and can be overcome only by curbing female desire and independence: Just as all the men must be protected or exonerated, so the women must be killed or imprisoned. On the one hand, Millhone could never identify with this threatening version of femininity and thus ensures that the women are punished and stability is restored; on the other, Millhone as daughter accepts her subordination within the father/daughter dyad. Thus, her primary identification with masculinity not only maintains gender as gender difference but also, in a contradictory and narratively conservative way, reinscribes gender as gender hierarchy. Even as she plays with gender difference by parodying both masculinity and (to a lesser extent) femininity, such playfulness fails as a disruptive strategy in the final analysis.

Where *F Is for Fugitive* defines gender in terms of individual psychology, *Blood Shot* locates it in social formations and resists rather than reinscribes gender hierarchy. The oppressive function of gender categories is clear in the way Warshawski is constructed by others—particularly the men she pursues—as an unnaturally unfeminine woman, a "bitch": mongrel bitch, cold-blooded bitch, meddlesome bitch. Such an epithet signals a need to reinforce femininity ("bitch" only applies to women) even as Warshawski's detective activities transgress the boundaries of proper femininity: Compliance, subservience, submission to the wills of men. It forcefully reinscribes Warshawski as female Other to the masculine Self, reasserting female inferiority through metaphors of animality even as the female detective acts to subvert and usurp male power.

Warshawski resists such constructions by locating an authentic and valorized female "Self" through her relations with strong female characters. Gabriella, Warshawski's deceased mother, exists in her memories as an accomplished opera singer and exemplary parent. Lotty, Warshawski's closest friend and mother-surrogate, is a renowned doctor who runs a family clinic for impoverished women and children. And Ms. Chigwell is a seventy-eight-year-old, fearless woman whose medical career was blocked by her gender but who becomes Warshawski's partner in a daring rescue.

These women, whose strength is *not* represented as traditionally "masculine," function as a community, homosocial in character and intensity, that mediates Warshawski's relationship to a tough world in which femaleness can be, if not a liability, then certainly an anomaly—a world in which she must rely on deception in order to succeed. Warshawski relates to each of them without deception or bravado, describing Lotty, for example, as "the one person I never lie to. She's—not my conscience—the person who helps me see who I really am, I guess" (BS 339). This authentic Self, constructed as female but not feminine within Warshawski's community, in turn enables her to defy the psychologized heterosexual binary that condemns feminity in *F Is for Fugitive*. Such a community, a crucial departure from the radically individualist male hard-boiled tradition, empowers Warshawski on a social level as she attacks the abuses of male power.

Paretsky, as opposed to Grafton, views incest within this political frame of male power. For Paretsky, incest signifies not a female desire that threatens the social order, but a male desire that constitutes it. Paretsky makes this argument structurally by overlaying two narratives—the search for Caroline Djiak's father and an investigation of industrial poisoning. Originally hired by Caroline, a childhood friend, to discover the identity of her father, Warshawski tries to trace some friends of Caroline's mother Louisa, who used to work at the Xerxes solvent plant. But these friends had died as a result of the chemical's toxicity, and Warshawski finds herself investigating a massive corporate cover-up.

This investigation leads to three powerful men—Humboldt, wealthy financier and owner of Xerxes; Dresberg, an organized crime boss; and Jurshak, a corrupt South Chicago politician. These three figures represent bastions of power, and Warshawski topples them all. She also discovers that Jurshak is the father of Caroline, whose mother Louisa was Jurshak's niece. Whereas the symbolically incestuous acts in Grafton are blamed on the daughters, here Jurshak is clearly responsible for the rape of his niece, part of a systematic pattern of abuse begun with Louisa's older sister.

The theme of the powerful abusing the powerless unites these stories of incest and corporate greed. By superimposing a crime of gender and a crime of class, Paretsky brings together the tales of two rapes: The rape of the girl's body by her uncle and the rape of workers' bodies by their employer. Both are performed by leading citizens who veil their culpability by allowing their victims to be blamed for their suffering: The pregnant Louisa was thrown out of the house to avoid scandal while the workers' illnesses were attributed to their smoking rather than their work environment.

Warshawski uncovers the truth behind these lies. This truth-bearing function is, of course, a central part of the traditional detective story, but here that function is radicalized. Classic detective narratives cleanse society by locating the source of disorder in specific deviant individuals who can be identified and purged, with the truth acting simultaneously to expose the criminal and to clear society as a whole (Cawelti 1976, 80-105; Taylor 1989). Paretsky's novels locate society's evils not on the margins but in its most central, stable figures. Her villains make up the pantheon of a male elite—politicians, corporate executives, bankers, union bosses, religious leaders. Nor are these villains deranged. Their motivations are inevitably financial, and their movement into crime is simply an extension of the logic of business.

This corrupt power lies not only in the public realm of business and politics but also in the private realm of the family. Thus, Warshawski physically or financially ruins Dresberg, Jurshak, and Humboldt; she also confronts Louisa's parents about disowning her. When Louisa's mother finally acknowledges the incest, her husband slaps her. Warshawski punches him in return, initiating a full-scale fight. "I stood over him panting from fury, my gun in my hand barrel-first, ready to smash it into him if he started to get up. His face was glazed—none of his women-folk had ever fought back against him" (BS 273).

Most significant here is not that Warshawski gets into a fight, a standard trope in hard-boiled fiction, but that she fights on behalf of women. The gun, barrel-first, is no longer Millhone's fetishized phallus, but a threatening bludgeon. Warshawski fights not so much like a man as like a fury, an avenging spirit striking out against malevolent uses of male power; and with such a gesture she transforms detection into political resistance. Grafton, accepting both gender opposition and hierarchy, offers no such social model; her individualism leads to a maintenance of the gendered status quo rather than social transformation. Paretsky, on the other hand, rethinks the detective's inscription in both social and gender hierarchies and offers a utopian social model grounded in values of authenticity and egalitarianism, a model in which women (and some men) emerge as a unified political force with a single, clear response to women's oppression.

She does so, however, at the expense of a critical examination of the construction of Warshawski's identity. Just as Warshawski's political utopia is a fiction, so too is any sense of authentic and unified "selfhood." Yet both fictions are necessary in the politics of Paretsky's work, which posits a feminist Archimedean point from which Warshawski can critique male power formations.

In this light, Grafton's epistemology of performance may be more politically useful in the long run, since her play with gender categories offers the possibility of their symbolic deconstruction. More recent works, Grafton's *H Is for Homicide* and the movie *V. I. Warshawski*, exhibit both the potential and the limitations of this more playful approach to gender.

Like *F Is for Fugitive*, *V. I. Warshawski*, a Disney film loosely based on two of Paretsky's novels, parodies gender categories and thus subverts Paretsky's more trenchant critiques of male power. In this film, Warshawski is firmly embedded in the heterosexual binary, her toughness treated as a cross-dressing joke. We first see her as she wakes up in her filthy apartment and sniffs her running clothes before putting them on; we then cut from the morning's jogging shoes to the evening's high heels. Clearly she occupies both masculine and feminine positions, but the borderline never blurs. The movie dispenses with Warshawski's female community while playing up her heterosexual attachments. Lottie is marginalized, while Murray Ryerson, Warshawski's reporter friend, becomes both central and romantic; and the narrative is set in motion when she picks up a man in a bar who is later murdered.

The plot of the film reinforces a conservative rather than an alternative social and familial vision. Warshawski seduces Boom-Boom Grafalk, a hockey star and part owner of a threatened shipping business; when he is murdered, she both takes care of his daughter Kat and investigates his death. The ultimate villain is Boom-Boom's ex-wife, now married to his dissolute brother. Identified by her loose morality (promiscuity, drug and alcohol dependency), she ultimately attempts to kill her own daughter to gain her inheritance. Warshawski thus is positioned on the side of the paternal bond against the bad mother, just as she is positioned on the side of corporate stability and inherited wealth against hedonistic criminals. Finally, Warshawski is established here on the side of mystification over truth. After killing Kat's mother, who is trying to drown her daughter, Warshawski asks Murray to print the report that the mother died trying to protect Kat. "You wouldn't want her growing up thinking her mother tried to kill her." In stark contrast to her decision to tell Caroline of her incestuous parentage, the filmic Warshawski lies to reinforce the ideology of the nuclear family. The film ends with the rebellious female detective reinserted in the family, as she and Murray take the place of Kat's now-dead parents.

Thus the film flips pronouns but ultimately maintains the structure and generic rules of the traditional thriller. Its gender switch acts as a joke, easily laughed off as one returns to the comfortable position of the nuclear family by the end. Yet, this bifurcation between stable opposites, this fragmentation of gender subjectivity, however regressive in the film and in *F Is for Fugitive*, has the potential to open a conceptual space for destabilizing "femininity" as such. *H Is for Homicide*, one of Grafton's later novels, suggests (despite its use of class and ethnic stereotypes) the possibility—however fragile—of a politics that binds rather than divides women, a politics dependent upon the instability of bourgeois ideological constructions of "femininity." "Woman" becomes pluralized into "women," differentiated by ethnicity and class but linked by shifting alliances born of the performative quality of gender.

One first encounters Millhone as she returns from Los Angeles in her VW bug at 3:00 A.M. to her cozy home, recently rebuilt by her landlord Henry Pitts. "Life was good," Millhone muses. "I was female, single, with money in my pocket and enough gas to get home. I had nobody to answer to and no ties to speak of" (HH 3). Soon, however, this self-assured Millhone goes under cover for most of the book as "Hannah Moore"—skintight pants, ratted hair, inexpert makeup, and cheap perfume abounding. "What a vamp . . . what a tramp!" Millhone chirps. "I didn't know I had it in me" (HH 48). This literal performance, this parodic persona of the trashy woman, complicates Grafton's already-destabilized gender categories as class becomes a marker of difference *within* "femininity."

"Hannah Moore" accompanies Bibianna Diaz, a woman Millhone's been tailing for auto insurance fraud, back to Los Angeles. Both are more or less abducted by Raymond Maldonado, a kingpin in the fraud industry and Diaz's viciously self-appointed fiance. In her initial interactions with Maldonado, Millhone experiences a kind of exhilaration at the freedoms of her newfound persona. "I was making up Hannah's character as I went along, and it was liberating as hell. She was short-tempered, sarcastic, outspoken and crude. I could get used to this. License to misbehave" (HH 125). This impertinent femininity allies her across class lines with Diaz, whom she tries to protect from Maldonado's advances and abuses.

But Hannah Moore's exaggerated femininity shifts as the book progresses from sass and trash to the vulnerability that also marks Diaz's relationship with Maldonado. As she finds herself trapped in a rundown apartment, making dubious friends with a pit bull, guarded constantly by one of Maldonado's men, no gun and no telephone to call for help, such discursive freedom feels hollow. This disempowered feminine position vis-à-vis male violence provokes a rupture in the text, an intense moment of homesickness. "I felt a squeezing in my stomach," she says, "not an ache, but some process that was almost like grief" (HH 212). Her thoughts slip back to childhood and a child's memories of the horrors of the first moments away from home at summer camp.

This return to home, the safe and comfortable space of the bourgeois, signifies both Millhone's need to escape the suffocation of a specifically gendered class position that she has come dangerously close to adopting and the conventional detective story's need for closure. The return is thus a gesture that provides haven for the individual while leaving unequal social relations intact: Millhone has an out, while Diaz may not. Still, in spite of the conservatism of the resolution, "Hannah Moore's" friendship with Diaz suggests the utopian possibilities of a postmodern approach to identity. Gender in this scheme cannot be contained within stable binary oppositions (masculine and feminine) based on either biology or equally shared oppression; gender categories are themselves decentered, creating the possibility of alliance by exposing the fictionality of a unity based on the erasure of ethnic and class difference.

Complicated questions thus arise about the implications of the gender strategies employed by Paretsky and Grafton. Is Paretsky's vision of authentic truth and justice a function of the epistemology of the detective story, which is built around the masculine paradigm of uncovering the single truth and achieving closure? Does Grafton's poststructuralist destabilization of gender categories have the potential to break out of those narrative conventions? Or is some form of realist epistemology an essential foundation for any substantive political critique and ultimately more powerful than a focus on discursive instability?

The academic paper, like the detective novel, is conventionally structured around the search for evidence, the weighing of hypotheses, the investigation of causation. And like the detective novel, the academic paper climaxes with the privileged understanding, the story that makes all the details fall into place. This paper does not conclude that way. Instead of suppressing the contradictory moments in collaborative writing, we wish to foreground them by breaking into our individual voices for a final commentary:

Timothy Shuker-Haines: While acknowledging the tremendous power of post-structuralist critiques of representation, I want to defend Paretsky's project and ultimately the very concept of closure. Any social critique, including feminism, that is going to remain politically substantive and generative must ground itself, at least implicitly, on a vision of what the world is and what it should be. An exclusive focus on strategies of representation would condemn feminism to academicism, aestheticism, and marginality. To critique oppression we must believe in an alternative justice; to critique falsehood, we must believe in some form of an alternative truth. Such concepts as truth and justice sound hopelessly bourgeois and masculine and are clearly potentially oppressive, but I think we implicitly believe in them; and we are shackling ourselves if we do not articulate them, offer a critique of them, and ultimately fight for them. I see this as Paretsky's project; I think it's a noble one.

Martha Umphrey: Yet it seems to me that, in the realm of fiction, politics and representational strategies are inseparable. Warshawski's sense of identity (at least Paretsky's version of it) is the vehicle for and epistemologically equatable with the sense of closure and catharsis offered in the detective story's generic structure. Thus, it may well be that the conservative ideology of form inhering in the detective story serves to contain as much as to liberate Paretsky's feminist politics. One key insight in current feminist theory, informed by post-structuralism and, I think, more importantly by critiques of "mainstream" feminism offered by women of color, is that just as subjectivity itself is multiple and fragmented, so too is the category of "woman." Closing down the play of meaning by fixing it in the unproblematized identity of a single woman, a female detective, appears in that light as potentially regressive; and thus Grafton's strategies for destabilizing subjectivity appear at least potentially more promising as a means of politicizing the genre than Paretsky's. It's possible, as Gertrude Stein wrote of her own mystery *Blood on the Dining Room Floor*, that "on the whole a detective story does have to have an ending" (Stein 1982, 88) (and, one might add, a detective); but if so, then to perform feminist cultural work that is potentially liberating for all women, the very form of the detective narrative may have to dissolve, as has this essay, into nonresolution.

NOTES

1. This figure is not the only type of classic female detective, but she remains one of the best known. For surveys of female detectives, see Kline (1988), Craig and Cadogan (1981), and Reddy (1988).

2. Cawelti (1986) remains a crucial work in analyzing classic and hard-boiled detective fiction.

3. For the most popularized, although problematic because potentially essentializing, analysis of femininity as relational, see Gilligan (1982).

4. Quotations from the novels are cited in the text using the following abbreviations:

FF: Sue Grafton's *F Is for Fugitive* (1990)
HH: Sue Grafton's *H Is for Homicide* (1991)
BS: Sara Paretsky's *Blood Shot* (1988).

5. For an extended theoretical discussion of gender as performative, see Butler (1990).

6. For a summary of theory on the disruptiveness of female sexuality, see E. Ann Kaplan (1980).

REFERENCES

Butler, Judith. *Gender Trouble: Feminism and the Subversion of Identity*. New York: Routledge, 1990.

Cawelti, John. *Adventure, Mystery, and Romance: Formula Stories as Art and Popular Culture*. Chicago: University of Chicago Press, 1976.

Craig, Patricia, and Mary Cadogan. *The Lady Investigates: Women Detectives and Spies in Fiction*. London: Victor Gollancz, 1981.

Gilligan, Carol. *In a Different Voice: Psychological Theory and Women's Development*. Cambridge, MA: Harvard University Press, 1982.

Glover, David. "The Stuff That Dreams Are Made of: Masculinity, Femininity and the Thriller." In *Gender, Genre, and Narrative Pleasure*, edited by Derek Longhurst, 67-83. London: Unwin Hyman, 1989.

Grafton, Sue. *F Is for Fugitive*. New York: Henry Holt and Company, 1989. Reprint.

New York: Bantam, 1990.

____. *H Is for Homicide*. New York: Henry Holt and Company, 1991.

Hirsch, Foster. *The Dark Side of the Screen: Film Noir*. San Diego, CA: A. S. Barnes, 1981.

Kaplan, E. Ann. "Introduction." In *Women in Film Noir*, edited by E. Ann Kaplan, 1-5. London: British Film Institute Publishing, 1980.

Kline, Kathleen. *The Woman Detective: Gender and Genre*. Urbana: University of Illinois Press, 1988.

Paretsky, Sara. *Blood Shot*. New York: Delacorte, 1988. Reprint. New York: Dell, 1989.

Place, J. A., and L. S. Peterson. "Some Visual Motifs of Film Noir." In *Movies and Methods: An Anthology*, edited by Bill Nichols, 325-38. Berkeley: University of California Press, 1976.

Reddy, Maureen. *Sisters in Crime: Feminism and the Crime Novel*. New York: Continuum, 1988.

Schrader, Paul. "Notes on Film Noir." In *Film Genre Reader*, edited by Barry Keith Grant, 169-82. Austin: University of Texas Press, 1986.

Stein, Gertrude. *Blood on the Dining Room Floor*. Alice B. Toklas, 1948. Reprint. Berkeley, CA: Creative Arts Book Company, 1982.

Taylor, Barry. "*Gorky Park*: American Dreams in Siberia." In *Gender, Genre, and Narrative Pleasure*, edited by Derek Longhurst, 136-56. London: Unwin Hyman, 1989.

II

The Detective in Film and Television

Detectives appear early in the existence of film and television. Although the classic detectives of literature were the subjects of numerous adaptations (which may be the primary means by which the general populace knows about them), subversions of the formulas started well before Hollywood gave its imprimatur to the genre in the 1930s. Louis Feuillade's *Fantomas* series (1913-14), for example, emphasizes the master villain rather than his foe, Inspector Juve. Nevertheless, any survey of the detective in film and television reveals a pattern similar to that of literary predecessors: a classic hero who becomes parodied to some extent and subverted as the genre evolves. The five essays that follow explore aspects of this pattern in film but also suggest that the television detective is on his or her way to being subverted as well.

In her essay on Hollywood's process of adaptation, Meri-Jane Rochelson demonstrates how a penetrating look at the Victorian social fabric in Israel Zangwill's *The Big Bow Mystery* becomes a confirmation of a complacent social order in Don Siegel's *The Verdict*. Moreover, the attributes of the stereotypical Victorian detective (probably best known through Basil Rathbone's Sherlock Holmes), generally accepted to be fundamental to the genre, may well be the result of Hollywood's creation of a Victorian mise-en-scène. Zangwill's novel presents a very different picture of class struggles, flophouses, and labor strife. As with its other adaptations of nineteenth-century novels, Hollywood chose to resolve detective fiction on the side of "reassuring moral conclusions" rather than "by an ending that undermines conventional moral certainties."

James Maxfield's interrogation of Roman Polanski's *Chinatown*, however, shows what a difference a couple of decades can make, for Polanski uses the characteristics of the classic detective to subvert them and to produce a world with virtually no moral center. Jake Gittes may *look* like the 1930s hard-boiled detective, the man of action, but he proves throughout the film that he is the opposite. And the end of the film demonstrates a "bleak philosophical perspective" about a world in which "evil is ineradicable." The detective not only cannot overcome evil; he contributes to its victory.

Joel and Ethan Coen's *Miller's Crossing* may not at first seem to be a detective film, but Katherine Restaino's comparison of it with Dashiell Hammett's *The Glass Key* reveals links that make the film a modern (maybe even a postmodern) exemplar of the genre. Exploring the bleakness that pervades the Continental Op's world, Restaino shows how that world is present in the Coens' film and how *Miller's Crossing*, like *Chinatown*, chooses ambiguity and despair rather than traditionally positive narrative closure to solve its mysteries.

Although *The Thin Man*, a late 1950's television series, was an adaption of another Hammett novel (as had been an earlier film series), the television detective has very often been an original—but strongly dependent on earlier models. The final two essays examine an original series and an adapted series. Jan Whitt's comparison of Poe's Auguste Dupin with Jessica Fletcher, the protagonist of *Murder, She Wrote*, reveals that a late-twentieth-century female detective has much in common with one of the genre's essential paradigms. Paying attention to the "very simplicity" of the evidence, both detectives divulge information by confiding it to a confidante, demonstrate their detection skills to be superior to those of an official investigator, and possess an uncanny ability to "know something about people." The social order is restored in Jessica Fletcher's world, as it was in Dupin's.

J. Dennis Bounds confirms the formulaic nature of the genre with his analysis of *Perry Mason*, but he also provides insight into the working method of this particular series. By delving into the Erle Stanley Gardner papers at the University of Texas, Bounds shows how Gardner himself worked to maintain the formula while at the same time varying it in order to maintain audience interest. The series' two-movement narrative structure became the means for its long-lived set of principles (principles that were in evidence even when substitutes took over the courtroom for Mason on occasion); moreover, by comparing *Perry Mason* with *Columbo* and *The Rockford Files*, two subsequent series, Bounds clarifies the way genres endure by employing the formula/variation approach. The detective on television may not yet have reached the evolutionary stage of self-reflexivity and parody that the detective novel or the detective film has, but the seeds of that stage are certainly present in current series, and time awaits the postmodern heirs of Perry Mason and Jessica Fletcher.

8

Bending the Bow: *The Verdict* (1946) and the Hollywood Victorian Detective

Meri-Jane Rochelson

For two weeks in 1891, readers of the daily *London Star* were treated to *The Big Bow Mystery*, the first and only detective novel by Israel Zangwill, a Jewish journalist and humor writer, who in the next year, with his novel *Children of the Ghetto*, would become an Anglo-Jewish celebrity with a trans-Atlantic following. *The Big Bow Mystery* itself combines a satire of current social and artistic trends with what has been called "one of the best of the 'crime in a sealed room' problems" (Murch 151) and "the first significant story to be based solidly and solely on the concept of the locked room" (Bleiler in Zangwill xv). The intriguing nature of the detective plot led to *The Big Bow Mystery*'s adaptation as three feature films: *The Perfect Crime* (1928), *The Crime Doctor* (1934), and *The Verdict* (1946). None of these films was completely faithful to the original; each of the first two dropped the Victorian setting while maintaining the essential details of the murder mystery. *The Verdict* (with a screenplay by Peter Milne, directed by Don Siegel, and featuring Sydney Greenstreet and Peter Lorre in their last film together) removed from Zangwill's story evidence of anxieties concerning social class, political movements, and the nature of good and evil themselves—all of which preoccupied late Victorian writers and readers. Instead, *The Verdict* presents a Victorianism of overstuffed chairs, heavy draperies, and reassuring moral conclusions, contributing to a stereotype that came to define not only the age for twentieth-century moviegoers but also the genre of classical English detective fiction. The film restored the Victorian ambience but in a way that reflected 1940s notions of Victorianism and heroism.

Current theories support stereotypes of Victorian detection. "In movie form," writes Robert Reiner, the "interest [of 'the classic detective story'] lies less in the puzzle element than in the evocation of a lifestyle of indolent luxury and froth" (199). Like Stevenson in *Dr. Jekyll and Mr. Hyde*, however, and Wilde in *The Picture of Dorian Gray*, writers of detective fiction in the late nineteenth century portrayed a much darker and more unsettling view of society than later readers and viewers expect—though that darkness tends to be further below the surface.[1] In Sherlock Holmes stories such as "The Sign of Four" and "The Five Orange Pips," for example, Conan Doyle provides an anticolonial subtext. In *The Big Bow Mystery*, too, attentive readers of a novel alternately humorous and ingenious find themselves shocked by an ending that undermines conventional moral certainties.

Zangwill's novel concerns the murder of Arthur Constant, a working-class leader of patrician origins, who is apparently found murdered in his bed in a Bow-district boardinghouse. His landlady, Mrs. Drabdump, makes the discovery in the company of her neighbor George Grodman, a retired police detective whom she has summoned after being unable to awaken her tenant. Constant's throat is found to have been slit with a razor that cannot be located, there is little blood in evidence though the gash is deep, and the doors and windows have all been bolted from the inside: Grodman must break down the door to enter. A coroner's inquest rules out suicide, and suspicion settles on Mrs. Drabdump's tenant Tom Mortlake, another labor leader and Constant's friend.

The case is pursued by Edward Wimp, Grodman's successor and former rival at Scotland Yard. Grodman allows Wimp to continue in a hopeless direction until it appears that Mortlake's alibi will not appear in time to save him from hanging—or to discredit Wimp's now-exalted reputation. At that point Grodman confesses to the Home Secretary: in "the desire to commit a crime that should baffle detection" (296) he killed Arthur Constant in the presence of Mrs. Drabdump, while she shielded her eyes as he broke down the door and cried out, "My God!" Grodman had counted on Mrs. Drabdump's assuming her boarder was dead when she could not wake him, and he had given Constant the sedative that would ensure a deep sleep. In a final irony, Grodman discovers after his confession that a letter proving Mortlake's innocence has already arrived, that the confession was not needed to exonerate him, and thus that Grodman's perfect crime would have remained unsolved. Learning this, Grodman kills himself on the spot.

Much in this story calls into question the commonly held assumption that Victorian detective fiction is conservative and reassuring.[2] The location of the detective's flat in a working-class neighborhood is in the first place a divergence from the image of the classical detective's genteel study, regardless of where the criminal investigation may lead him. In addition, although Zangwill at times uses humor to distance himself from working-class characters, the respect given their ideals and their leaders (both the victim, Constant, and the accused, Mortlake) conflicts with a pattern of dismissal that has been noted in other early detective fiction.[3] The nobility of the workers and the permanence of their cause is underscored in the final sentence of the novel, which stands alone as a paragraph: After Grodman falls dead, "[s]ome of the working men who had been standing waiting by the shafts of the hansom helped to bear the stretcher" (302).

Apart from evoking sympathy for the workers' cause, the plot of *The Big Bow Mystery* challenges readers' beliefs in more fundamental ways. Although Grodman is not officially the detective on the murder case, he seems to have the moral and intellectual qualities associated with the classic detective. Thus, the reader sees him as central and roots for him—and not for Wimp (who fills the role of "bumbling police investigator")—to solve the crime. When it turns out that Grodman himself is the murderer, not only is a classic rule of fair play violated,[4] but the very cold-bloodedness of the deed contradicts all the reader's confident and admiring assumptions about him. For example, Grodman's choice of Constant as victim is apparently motivated by nothing more than a combination of circumstances that make it convenient for Grodman to use him in a previously considered plan—although, in praising Constant's idealism, Grodman adds, "I felt instinctively he would be the man. . . . It is a pity humanity should have been robbed of so valuable a life" (297). Until his confession, the reader has evaluated Grodman according to assumptions encouraged by the conventions of the detective genre. To find these assumptions ungrounded and the murder unmotivated by any redeeming factor places the reader in a morally haphazard, uncertain universe. This is not reassuring.

Neither is the self-destructiveness of Grodman's confession. I have argued elsewhere that *The Big Bow Mystery* embeds a parable of ethnic anxiety, following the pattern of several of Zangwill's works on Jewish themes (Rochelson 11-20). Central to this pattern is the self-willed confession of identity, prompted by a need so powerful that, in Grodman's case, it prevents his inquiring about the cheers of workers he hears on his way to speak with the Home Secretary. Those cheers, unbeknownst to Grodman, are inspired by the news of Tom Mortlake's reprieve. The transformation of the brilliant and witty ex-detective into an amoral, diabolically clever, broken man leaves the reader without any bearings at the end of the novel. Zangwill underscores the moral ambiguity of this ending with what he may have conceived as a private joke: The name "Grodman" in Yiddish means "straight," "even," or "right" man (Weinreich).

Names are not a bad place to begin in examining how the 1946 *The Verdict* transformed Zangwill's novel. While the conversion of Mrs. Drabdump to Mrs. Benson and Edward Wimp to John Buckley may simply be a matter of twentieth-century tastes, other changes have more significant thematic implications. In place of the nobly named Arthur Constant there is Arthur Kendall, no longer a self-sacrificing leader of the workers' cause, but a patrician who has never left his comfortable fold. Tom Mortlake becomes Clive Russell, a member of Parliament who is a champion of the miners and Kendall's political enemy. He is quite clearly of the middle or upper class, however, and in fact must withhold his alibi because it involves one Lady Pendleton. The working-class Bow district setting disappears entirely, as Mrs. Benson's boardinghouse features a wide staircase with heavy banisters, spacious rooms, and elegant appointments. Both the staircase, on which shadowy figures rise and descend, and the heavy draperies, whose abundant swags often frame shots of the film, have a strong visual presence, asserting the opulence that surrounds Arthur Kendall, in particular. As Kendall retires to bed on the last night of his life, a close-up focuses on the jewelled tiepin he places next to his soon-to-be-extinguished candle. This is neither a manor house nor the most exclusive square in London; Mrs. Benson is also landlady to Grodman's companion and alter ego, an odd, young, foreign-accented artist of indeterminate social rank (Peter Lorre). But the effect is clearly and insistently, as John Cawelti has put it, one of "the rather snobbish upper-class settings that so often characterize the classical detective story" (99).

Ernest Haller's cinematography gives *The Verdict* the visual qualities of film noir. Zangwill's London fog is almost tangible; oblique lines (those staircase banisters) slice the screen and oblique camera angles herald such scenes as Superintendent Bentley's (incorrect) announcement of the murderer. Lighting is expressionistic, with extreme contrasts of light and shadow, especially in scenes of heavy drama or suspense. Near the end of the film, when Grodman hints at the true conclusion to a nervous and mournful Emmrich—and the viewer may be led to believe that Emmrich is the killer—the background interior is murky as the characters' faces move into and out of the light. There is even an added exhumation scene, whose turbid atmosphere is indeed more gothic than noir. Frederick Hollander's music contributes to the mournful tension and foreboding. Despite these elements of style, however, changes in details of the plot—the most dramatic differences from Zangwill's novel—remove from *The Verdict*, on a thematic level, the "confusion and . . . instability" of film noir (Nachbar 67). The 1946 film, in fact, neatly ties the epistemological and moral loose ends of its Victorian precursor.

Some of the changes may be related to the values of the Motion Picture Production Code then in force. In the film, Kendall is killed with a knife to the heart, as opposed to Constant's rather more messy throat-slitting; the murder is shown in a silhouette flashback. Denzil Cantercot, a poet-aesthete at the center of a comic subplot in Zangwill's novel, is replaced by the artist Victor Emmrich (Lorre), who, like his predecessor, assists Grodman (Greenstreet) in writing his memoirs. Cantercot's bigamy, a silly red herring in the novel, is replaced in the film by a rather improbable flirtation between Emmrich and Kendall's former girlfriend, a music-hall singer. It is hard not to conclude that the main purpose of this diversion is to confirm Emmrich's uncomplicated heterosexual orientation, given his devotion to Grodman and somewhat "perverse" mannerisms (to use the Production Code language), including an expressed excitement as Kendall's body is exhumed.[5] The most significant changes from novel to film, however, are in the murder plot and its motivation. Whether inspired by Production Code mores or not, these change the very nature of the work.

One of the most shocking facts about the murder of Zangwill's Constant is that his murderer liked and admired him. He was, by Grodman's own admission, a just and noble man, whose death was a loss to humanity. No good purpose was served by it, no wrong set right, and it occurred solely through an act of intellectual vengeance, Grodman's desire to foil his rival's attempt to solve the mystery. *The Verdict*'s Grodman also wishes to foil Superintendent Buckley (George Coulouris), who succeeded him after the wrong man was convicted in the murder of Arthur Kendall's aunt. As the viewer learns at the end of the film, however, Kendall himself killed his aunt Hannah, and, as Grodman reveals, "He not only killed his aunt but he had knowingly permitted an innocent man to hang for his crime." If Russell had not been convicted (and there was no hard evidence against him), Grodman's unsolved murder of Kendall would have humiliated Buckley and at the same time caused justice to be done. That Grodman sees himself as an agent of justice is reinforced explicitly when he adds, of Kendall, "He was a double murderer. There was no other way to bring him to book."

The circumstances of the two confessions also produce two very different Grodmans. In *The Big Bow Mystery*, it is as if the ex-detective is impelled to confess and to reveal, almost with pride, his true criminality. Like *The Verdict*'s Grodman, he has made extensive efforts to locate the accused man's alibi (although, unlike the Sydney Greenstreet character, he does not personally travel through France to Monte Carlo). However, when he hears the cheering crowds outside the Home Secretary's office, he fails to ask about the celebration, and as they cheer because the alibi has turned up, he seems to take for granted that they are cheering because he will exonerate Mortlake. Thus Grodman fails to learn, in time, that Mortlake has been reprieved. Depriving the law of its final rights in this case, Grodman shoots himself in the heart after learning from the Home Secretary that "Mr. Wimp's card-castle would have tumbled to pieces without your assistance" (302). When *The Verdict*'s Grodman confesses, however, he actually saves Russell, since Lady Pendleton, who alone could have proved the alibi, has died. Grodman reaches the prison, in heavy fog, just four hours before the scheduled execution. After his confession he walks toward the prison, as the camera pans vertically to the top of a church tower where a bell tolls. Presumably, justice will be done by the authorities; self-destruction has become self-sacrifice.

The revision of *The Big Bow Mystery* in twentieth-century film "Victorianizes" detective fiction, as Hollywood had similarly revised disturbing examples of other late-nineteenth-century genres. In Albert Lewin's 1945 film *The Picture of Dorian Gray*, for example, Dorian rejects Sybil Vane not because her acting suffers when she falls in love (the reason Wilde ascribes to his aestheticist hero), but rather because she has spent the night with him. This explanation, entirely out of character for both Dorian Gray and Oscar Wilde, presumably conforms to viewers' notions of Victorian morality, but it also creates and perpetuates such notions. Similarly, most film versions of *The Strange Case of Dr. Jekyll and Mr. Hyde* add a central sympathetic female character (Wexman 284), which both diffuses the novel's atmosphere of intense male clubbiness and limits the arena of Hyde's vice to the heterosexual. Apart from the influence of the

Production Code, the pattern of such changes suggests a desire by a younger generation to view its predecessors as innocent, naive, or simply old-fashioned. In ascribing a clear-cut, simple morality to its Victorian forebears, Hollywood filmmakers and their audience are able to assert their own greater complexity and open-mindedness while at the same time finding reassurance in the idea of a stable past. Rereading the original Victorian texts, however, shows this comfort to be illusory.

In *The Verdict*, the possible diminishment of the original novel is reflected in Bosley Crowther's review comment that "[i]t is rather hard to figure just what the Warners saw in this antique mystery story" (29) and, in one of the few recent references to the film, Bernard Drew's categorization of it as, simply, "[a] Victorian whodunit" (24). Still, although in taming the unsettling ending of *The Big Bow Mystery* Siegel and Milne conformed and contributed to stereotypes of Victorianism, their Grodman is not without his own fascination. *The Verdict* was the first feature directed by Siegel, who went on to gain renown with, among other films, *Riot in Cell Block 11* (1954), *Invasion of the Body Snatchers* (1956), *Baby Face Nelson* (1957), and *Dirty Harry* (1971). Colin McArthur writes that "Siegel's view of the world presupposes his heroes' rejection of or by a timorous and nondescript society" (150), a definition that seems to fit—though differently in each case—both Zangwill's and Siegel's Grodman.[6] No longer officially a part of the police fraternity, each commits a criminal act that both defies judicial norms and asserts (if only inwardly) his intellectual superiority to the police force and to society at large. But while Grodman's confession and suicide in *The Big Bow Mystery* horrify readers with the sense of their own misreading of character, the Grodman of Siegel's film, as portrayed by Sydney Greenstreet, fits into a well-known and admired twentieth-century character type. He is very much the loner, living apparently within society but in fact outside it, acting according to his own code but nobly submitting when necessary.

As *The Verdict* leaves intact its viewers' sense of a just universe, a complex, tragic victim/villain becomes a tragic hero. Grodman, in his last line of dialogue, remarks to Emmrich that whether or not he has "done deeds of calculated and unfathomable villainy . . . will probably remain an open verdict." Despite the tantalizing possibility this suggests, it is clear that the film departs from Zangwill's disturbing conclusion. A bit of thought reminds the viewer that Emmrich has already read the earlier parts of Grodman's memoirs; it is only the last chapter he trembles at seeing. The film's title persuades that the verdict is clear. Grodman remains an "upright man"—the one character whose name does not change in this transformation of novel to film.

NOTES

I wish to thank my former student Ty Forbes for his generous technical assistance in this project.

1. In *Film and the Narrative Tradition*, John L. Fell lists an impressive number of novels from the 1880s and 1890s incorporating bizarre transformations (79). Fell cites them as early examples of unusual "visual" effects, but, as he also suggests, they are also evidence of psychological and epistemological sophistication.

2. For just a few examples of this view, see John G. Cawelti, *Adventure, Mystery, and Romance: Formula Stories as Art and Popular Culture*, 101-5; Dennis Porter, *The Pursuit of Crime: Art and Ideology in Detective Fiction*, 120-29; and Mark Freiman, "Structure and Ideology in the Classical British Detective Story."

3. See Jeanne F. Bedell, "Melodrama and Manners: Changing Attitudes toward Class Distinctions in English Detective Fiction, 1868-1939."

4. "The detective must not himself commit the crime" is one of the items in the "Detective Decalogue" of Father Knox, summarized by Julian Symons in *The Detective Story in Britain*, Bibliographical Series of Supplements to "British Book News" on Writers and Their Work, general ed. Bonamy Dobree (London: Longmans, 1962), 22.

5. Lorre's strangeness is in fact one of the delights of the film. One of my favorite moments occurs when he enters the boardinghouse and startles the high-strung Mrs. Benson, who blurts out, "Oh, it's you, Mr. Emmrich." Calmly, Lorre answers, "Yes, I think it's me"—and then checks in the mirror: "Yes, it is."

6. McArthur's definition (which, he notes, is derived from Alan Lovell's pamphlet *Don Siegel: American Cinema*) goes on to mention "their attempts to find an identity within a violent and hierarchic organization . . . [although] his heroes' explosive, even psychotic temperament frequently brings them into conflict with their organizations" (150-52; illustration 151). While such "conflict" to some extent plays a part in the story at hand, this part of the definition more clearly refers to Siegel's more hard-boiled protagonists.

REFERENCES

Bedell, Jeanne F. "Melodrama and Manners: Changing Attitudes toward Class Distinctions in English Detective Fiction, 1868-1939." *Clues: A Journal of Detection* 1, no. 1 (1980): 15-24.

Cawelti, John G. *Adventure, Mystery, and Romance: Formula Stories as Art and Popular Culture*. Chicago: University of Chicago Press, 1976.

Crowther, Bosley. "The Screen: Unimportant Question." *New York Times*, December 13, 1946, 29.

Drew, Bernard. "The Man Who Paid His Dues." *American Film* 3, no. 3 (December 1977/ January 1978): 22-27.

Fell, John L. *Film and the Narrative Tradition*. Norman: University of Oklahoma Press, 1974.

Freiman, Mark. "Structure and Ideology in the Classical British Detective Story." *Culture and Context* 1 (1980): 56-74.

McArthur, Colin. *Underworld U.S.A.* New York: Viking, 1972.

Murch, A. E. *The Development of the Detective Novel*. London: Peter Owen, 1958.

Nachbar, Jack. "Film Noir." In *Handbook of American Film Genres*, edited by Wes D. Gehring. Westport, CT: Greenwood Press, 1988.

Porter, Dennis. *The Pursuit of Crime: Art and Ideology in Detective Fiction*. New Haven, CT: Yale University Press, 1981.

Reiner, Robert. "Keystone to Kojak: The Hollywood Cop." In *Cinema, Politics and Society in America*, edited by Philip Davies and Brian Neve. New York: St. Martin's Press, 1981.

Rochelson, Meri-Jane. "*The Big Bow Mystery*: Jewish Identity and the English Detective Novel." *Victorian Review* 17, no. 2 (1991).

Weinreich, Uriel. *Modern English-Yiddish Yiddish-English Dictionary*. New York: Schocken, 1977.

Wexman, Virginia Wright. "Horrors of the Body: Hollywood's Discourse on Beauty and Rouben Mamoulian's *Jekyll and Mr. Hyde*." In *Dr. Jekyll and Mr. Hyde after One Hundred Years*, edited by William Veeder and Gordon Hirsch. Chicago: University of Chicago Press, 1988.

Zangwill, Israel. *The Big Bow Mystery*. In *Three Victorian Novels: The Unknown Weapon by Andrew Forrester; My Lady's Money by Wilkie Collins; The Big Bow Mystery*, edited by E. F. Bleiler. New York: Dover, 1978.

9

"The Injustice of It All": Polanski's Revision of the Private Eye Genre in *Chinatown*

James Maxfield

Aside from being filmed in color, Roman Polanski's *Chinatown* looks much like a classic 1940s detective film, and the protagonist Jake Gittes seems the typical hard-boiled, wisecracking private eye. But such resemblances ultimately turn out to be superficial: *Chinatown* echoes certain characteristic features of the classic detective film not to emulate but to subvert them. For instance, as in numerous detective films there is a confrontation scene in *Chinatown* in which the detective, Jake Gittes, faces the murderer, Noah Cross, one-on-one, with the evidence of his guilt. Such scenes almost invariably culminate in the villain being either arrested or killed by the detective, but in *Chinatown*, Gittes passively allows Cross's henchman not only to disarm him but to take away from him the only physical evidence of the murderer's presence at the scene of the crime. The film ends with the villain triumphant, the hero defeated, and the heroine dead—the expected ending of a detective film turned completely upside down.

Screenwriter Robert Towne had apparently written a more traditional ending, which director Polanski refused to accept. Polanski writes in his autobiography,

Towne wanted the evil tycoon to die and his daughter, Evelyn, to live. . . . I knew that if *Chinatown* was to be special, not just another thriller where the good guys triumph in the final reel, Evelyn had to die. Its dramatic impact would be lost unless audiences left their seats with a sense of outrage and the injustice of it all. (348)

The pessimism of the film's ending actually derives from more than Evelyn's death; however, because her demise is at the center of all that goes wrong in the final moments, it does serve as an emblem of the bleak philosophical perspective that underlies *Chinatown*: the notions that evil is ineradicable, events are uncontrollable and cannot be foreseen, and life can be snuffed out in an instant.

The film in an almost didactic manner teaches these "truths" to its protagonist Jake Gittes—and through him, to the audience. It is significant, though, that Gittes has been taught this lesson before; the film for him constitutes not so much a learning as a relearning experience. As a policeman in Chinatown, Gittes was taught that he couldn't "always tell what's going on" and that his attempts to produce one kind of result could very well create the opposite. When Gittes begins his investigation for the false Mrs. Mulwray, he attends a city council meeting at which a proposed dam is being discussed. Hollis Mulwray, testifying for the water and power commission, says that the new dam would be built on shale similar to that under the Van der Lip Dam, which "gave way," causing "over five hundred lives [to be] lost." He had approved that dam, but says, "I'm not going to make the same mistake twice." After this statement the film cuts to a close-up of Gittes in the audience. Later, when he tells Evelyn Mulwray about his experiences in Chinatown, Gittes has the opportunity to make the same kind of statement Hollis had made at the hearing, but he does not. In truth Gittes fully deserves the comment Lieutenant Escobar (his former partner in Chinatown) makes to him shortly before the end of the film: "You never learn, do you, Jake?" (But such is the cynicism of the film that Hollis Mulwray, the man who did learn his lesson, receives as his reward only an early death at the hands of Noah Cross.)

Chinatown opens with a scene only peripherally related to its central plot: Gittes's informing a lower-class client, Curly, of his wife's infidelity. The initial images are black-and-white stills of a man and woman having sexual intercourse. On the sound track there are moans, which at first seem associated with the love-making couple but which turn out to be the anguished response of the cuckolded husband, who then flings the photos in the air, lurches (sobbing) about the detective's office, and finally winds up with his face pressed against the window blinds. The introduction to Jake Gittes occurs when he coolly tells Curly not to "eat" the Venetian blinds because he "just had 'em installed on Wednesday." When Curly bitterly announces that his wife is "no good," Jake placidly agrees: "What can I tell you, kid? You're right. When you're right, you're right." He then eases Curly out of the office.

This scene immediately establishes that Jake Gittes is no idealistic private eye, like Philip Marlowe, who refuses to do divorce work. The repetition of "you're right" seems to suggest both a boundless cynicism about the morality of women (are any of them any good?) and an extremely limited empathy for Curly's feelings (as does the comment about the blinds). That Gittes ushers Curly out of the office without pressing any demand for payment seems less an act of kindness than the manifestation of a desire to be quickly rid of an annoyingly distraught client. When we later learn of Jake's experiences in Chinatown, we can retrospectively interpret his behavior in this opening scene and in much of the rest of the film as a defensive strategy: By regarding other people cynically or not caring too much about their feelings, he protects himself from disillusionment or from painful involvement with others.

In the following scene, when the false "Mrs. Mulwray" asks Gittes to find out if her husband is being unfaithful to her, he asks her, "do you love your husband?" When she replies that she does, he advises her to "go home, forget everything"—and that counsel could be interpreted as an attempt to spare the woman the suffering Curly has experienced through the certain knowledge of his mate's infidelity. But it may only be Jake's standard ploy with women wanting to have their husbands investigated—a way of warding off customer dissatisfaction when an inquiry produces dismaying results. In any case, he is willing enough to take the case when she insists, "I have to know!"

Jake treats the actual investigation more or less as a game—a game he is confident he has won when he manages to take photos of Mulwray with a girl in a boat on the lake at Echo Park and on a veranda at the El Macondo Apartments. The name of the park has symbolic resonance because *Chinatown* is full of echoes, the most obvious one being the echo of Gittes's earlier experience in Chinatown in the final sequence of the film. When Gittes is photographing Mulwray and the girl from a vantage point on the roof of the El Macondo, there is a reflection of the subjects in his camera's lens. The shot might remind the viewer of an earlier one in which Gittes observed Mulwray through the reflection in the circular, rearview mirror on the side of his car.

The film's emphasis on reflected images is another way of stressing the echo effect: Just as people and events are duplicated in their mirror reflections, so Evelyn Mulwray, for instance, duplicates the woman in Chinatown Jake tried "to keep . . . from being hurt" but only "ended up making sure that she was hurt." But when he photographs Mulwray and the girl from high above them on the rooftop, Gittes is unaware of the echoes or reflections he will later encounter. The structure of the shot suggests his sense of himself as someone who is on top of things—who has done his job and done it well. His first fall of the film occurs in the barbershop sequence immediately thereafter.

Although he didn't expect it, Gittes at first seems perfectly content to see the result of his investigation spread across the front page of an L.A. newspaper—that is, until another man in the barbershop makes a slighting comment. Gittes erupts in response to what he regards as an imputation to his professional honor, his defense partly taking the form of a counterattack: After he finds out that his critic works in the mortgage department of a bank, he snarls, "I don't kick families out of their houses like you bums down at the bank do!" He also asserts, "I make an honest living"—a statement he then repeats in an increasingly fragmentary manner: "make an honest living, . . . an honest living." The repetition, of course, only creates the impression of a man who "doth protest too much."

His second fall occurs in the next sequence when the real Evelyn Mulwray walks into his office behind him as he is telling his associates the dirty joke about the man who screwed "like a Chinaman." His embarrassment in telling such a story in the presence of a lady is nothing in comparison to that of discovering that he was deceived by a phony client. From this point on, he seeks to find out who had used him to discredit Mulwray—not merely for the purpose of defending himself from Mrs. Mulwray's lawsuit (which she tells him she will "drop" even before her husband's body is found), but more important to prove to himself that he is indeed "an honest man."

In the self-motivated investigation that follows, Gittes finds that the seemingly irrelevant parts of his previous observation of Hollis Mulwray's daily activities are now the relevant parts. After Mulwray's body is found in the Oak Pass Reservoir, his activities at various water sites about the city become clues to someone's motives for murdering him. Gittes slowly comes to the conclusion that Mulwray was murdered for two main reasons: because he was opposed to the new Alto Vallejo Dam and because he had discovered that water was being diverted to the Northwest Valley, thereby increasing the severity of the water shortage in Los Angeles.

Not only is water the motive for Mulwray's murder and the means of it (he is first thought to have drowned in the reservoir, but Gittes later discovers he met his death in the tidal pool in his own yard), it also poses a threat to Jake Gittes as well. When Hollis Mulwray is still alive, Gittes watches him down on the shore from a vantage point just in front of the opening of a big drainage pipe. Suddenly Gittes hears a sound of running water and just barely manages to jump aside as a runoff hurtles by him, slightly splashing him but just missing knocking him off the cliff on to the rocky beach below. He is less lucky when he visits the Oak Pass Reservoir at night after Mulwray's death. He hears shots, jumps down into a flood-control channel to get out of the way, and is crouching there when a surge of water pours onto him, sweeping him down channel until he is slammed up against a chain-link fence, which he barely manages to climb up and over to avoid drowning. Dismayed by the loss of a new "Florsheim shoe," he is limping along muttering to himself when he encounters Mulvihill, the corrupt former sheriff, and the small thug (played by director Polanski) who slits the detective's nose with a switchblade knife to warn him not to be "nosy."

The loss of the shoe, even though it may seem minor in comparison to the slashed nose, is a significant event in this sequence. When the body of Hollis Mulwray was dragged up from the reservoir, one of his shoes was missing also. The fact that Gittes has almost drowned as Mulwray did and has lost a shoe as he had, indicates the detective is following in Mulwray's footsteps. Certainly the violence done to his nose makes Gittes want to take up Mulwray's causes—to block the new dam and expose the diversion of water. But his identification with Mulwray goes beyond espousal of the man's causes; he also winds up in bed with Mrs. Mulwray.

The slashed nose, though, is more directly important as a motivation. The cutting of the nose becomes a symbolic castration. Gittes's sense of his manhood must have suffered a severe blow as he knelt holding his bloody nose while Mulvihill and the diminutive knife-wielder stood over him. Certainly, it is noticeable at this point in the film that Gittes does not put up the kind of fight against his adversaries expected from Sam Spade or Philip Marlowe; he just stands there and lets Mulvihill hold him while a man much smaller than he is carves him like an unresisting hunk of meat. Even the vengeance he fantasizes against the superiors of Mulvihill and the thug ("the big boys") is not the sort of manly action one expects from a tough private eye: He wants to "sue" them. In allowing his nose to be cut and in bearing the marks of this humiliation throughout the rest of the film, J. J. Gittes has suffered a loss that he can make up for only through virile action in his subsequent endeavors. The problem is that if he continues to try to assert himself, continues to be "nosy" as the thug put it, he runs the risk of not just partial, but total loss: As the thug warned, "Next time, you lose the whole thing"—as he in some sense does at the end of the film.

Jake manages to restore his sense of manhood for a time through two forms of behavior: violent risk-taking and sexual involvement. When he sees a "KEEP OUT NO TREPASSING" [sic] sign at the entrance to an orchard, he drives right in. Nor does he "Hold it right there" when this command follows a warning shot at his car; instead he guns it and goes roaring off down a lane between trees. When his path is blocked, he backs up and turns down another lane, finally coming to a stop only when holes have been shot in his radiator and tires—and he runs into a tree. Confronted by a group of enraged farmers, he makes little attempt to calm them down; he denounces one as a "dumb Okie" and winds up being knocked unconscious. He has put up a more vigorous resistance here than he did against Mulvihill and the thug, but the results have scarcely been better. Only the decency of the farmers, who have no wish to inflict further injury on a man who has been lying unconscious for several hours, and the arrival of Evelyn Mulwray, who has been summoned as his employer of record, get Jake out of the orchard without suffering additional damage.

But the next sequence at the Mar Vista Rest Home allows Gittes to restore his view of himself as a man who is on top of events and can dominate his adversaries when necessary. He makes a significant step in his investigation by discovering that land in the valley has been bought up in huge quantities in the names of unknowing residents of the home; and when he is confronted by Mulvihill in the lobby of the home, Gittes is able to pull the larger man's coat over his head and pound him into submission. He then avoids a further confrontation with the small thug and another henchman when Evelyn drives up just in time to whip him away from their menace. Nevertheless, his triumph over Mulvihill seems enough to restore his self-confidence and make him ready to demonstrate his manhood in another way—with Evelyn in bed.

Just as J. J. Gittes is not quite the classic hard-boiled private eye of earlier films, so Evelyn Mulwray is not quite the femme fatale of those films (nor the "good woman" who sometimes appears in order to balance her). When she first enters Gittes's office—cool, poised, beautiful—she seems to be the stock character expected in private eye films: "In almost every case, the hardboiled hero encounters a beautiful and dangerous woman in the course of his investigations and finds himself very much drawn to her, even to the point of falling in love" (Cawelti 186). In *Chinatown* Gittes *is* drawn to Evelyn—and toward the end may come to love her—but although she does prove to be extremely dangerous to him, it is not at all in the same way that the villainous women of earlier detective films were dangerous. Evelyn Mulwray is dangerous not because she is cool, hard, and ruthless but because she is neurotic, insecure, and vulnerable.

Her behavior in her first appearance in Gittes's office is misleading. Each successive time that Gittes talks to her the self-control Evelyn displayed in their first meeting breaks down a little more. Initially she speaks like a well-rehearsed actress delivering her lines in a drawing-room comedy, but when Gittes confronts her in later scenes, she becomes increasingly less fluent, groping for replies to his probing questions. (According to Polanski, this manifestation of the inner uncertainty of the character was aided by Faye Dunaway's inability to remember her lines [351].) Then her poise seems almost totally broken down when with shaking hands she lights a second cigarette—unaware she already has one going—after Gittes asks her a question about her father. And, of course, the ultimate breakdown comes when she admits in broken phrases that her sister is also her daughter. At that point the reason for her nervousness at the mention of her father's name becomes completely clear.

If one considers the film carefully, very little can actually be determined about Evelyn Cross Mulwray, her life, or her motives. First of all, did she know that her father had killed her husband? If not, why did she tell Gittes she was dropping her lawsuit against him (something that happens after Hollis is killed but before his body is discovered)? Later, after the body is found, why does she claim to the police that *she* had hired the detective to investigate her husband—why, if not to conceal the water plot that lies behind both the discrediting and the murder of her spouse? After Evelyn and Jake have made love, she warns him that her "father is a very dangerous man. You don't know how dangerous; you don't know how crazy." When Jake asks if Noah Cross could have killed her husband, she replies, "It's possible." If she does know or at least strongly suspects her father killed Hollis, did she initially try to deflect Gittes from finding that out in order to protect her father or simply because she assumed discovery of that fact would do neither Jake nor the public any good—since, as she says toward the end of the film, her father "owns the police" and therefore could never be brought to justice?

If Evelyn's knowledge of and motives in regard to the central crime of the film remain obscure, her sexual morality is also highly ambiguous. Was she really a promiscuous woman as she implied to Gittes in the restaurant scene? Did she really love her husband? Does she later love Gittes, or is she merely using sex to manipulate him into helping her defend her daughter? Even the incest with her father is presented ambiguously. When Gittes finally realizes the implications of Evelyn's insistence that Katherine is both her sister and her daughter, he places his own interpretation on that fact. He asks, obviously anticipating an affirmative answer, "He raped you?" Evelyn offers no verbal reply to the question, but she finally shakes her head briefly from side to side. Gittes wants to believe that she would not have committed incest unless brutally forced by her father, but her response offers no confirmation of this view and may even reject it.

In the screenplay for *Chinatown* (third draft), Evelyn explains to Gittes that her father "had a breakdown . . . the dam broke . . . my mother died . . . he became a little boy . . . I was fifteen . . . he'd ask me what to eat for breakfast, what clothes to wear! . . . it happened . . . then I ran away" (Towne 128). She also says she hates her father not for the incest itself but "for turning his back on [her] after it happened!" None of these lines appear in the finished film, possibly because the director deemed they went too far in mitigating Noah Cross's guilt; but neither does the movie offer any firm evidence that the incest occurred as the result of a rape rather than a seduction to which Evelyn at least half-willingly succumbed.

At any rate, Evelyn plainly feels that she was corrupted by her father, and she is willing to go nearly any lengths—even shooting him—to prevent him from having the same effect on their daughter Katherine. John Huston, as Evelyn's father Noah Cross, has been criticized for giving "an essentially, lazy unresonant performance opting for easy charm" (Simon 156), but the fact that he doesn't give an impression of obvious malignancy is one of the most chilling things about the character Noah Cross. Noah Cross is not so much *im*moral as utterly *a*moral. In regard to the incest he tells Gittes, "I don't blame myself. You see, Mr. Gits [sic], most people never have to face the fact that at the right time and right place, they're capable of anything." For him the act was simply normal human behavior produced by a particular confluence of circumstances. That Evelyn *does* blame him is merely a sign that she is, as he told Gittes earlier, "a disturbed woman." In Chinatown toward the end of the film, he can't understand why Evelyn won't "be reasonable" and turn Katherine over to him. After all, he is an old man and Katherine is his child as well as Evelyn's. He advised her, "Evelyn, you're a disturbed woman; you cannot hope to provide—." Although she shoots him at that moment, leaving uncertain what he thought Evelyn couldn't "provide," in the context of the introductory clause it seems most likely he meant that he, a sane man with a clear perspective on life, could give the girl the kind of stable existence she could never have with her neurotic mother. Evelyn's objections to him strike Noah as purely irrational.

Noah is as free of remorse for his killing of Hollis Mulwray as he is for the act of incest. Noah speaks fondly of Hollis as he stands beside the pool in which he drowned the man. He admits that Hollis's theories of water management "made this city." Unfortunately Hollis, with his opposition to the new dam, stood in the way of making the new city: the expanded Los Angeles that will incorporate the irrigated Northwest Valley. Hollis was fascinated with tidepools: "he used to say . . . that's where life begins." Hollis looked backward—to the origins of life and to the Van der Lip Dam disaster, a recurrence of which he sought to avoid in the future. Noah Cross looks to the future, willing to risk another disaster and willing to sacrifice his best friend to bring to fulfillment his vision of the new Los Angeles. As for the present, he feels as little guilt about diverting water from farmers who currently need it as he did about diverting his seed to his own daughter.

The film ends with the triumph of Noah Cross. The bullet wound he has received bothers him little more than would a bee sting as he leads his granddaughter/daughter away from the car in which her mother lies dead. The bleakness of the ending of the film is best understood by comparing it with an ending that screenwriter Robert Towne wrote but that the director chose not to use. In his autobiography, Polanski writes only of the "happy ending" Towne originally wanted (348), but the third draft of the screenplay contains a tragic ending that, nevertheless, offers possibilities of hope. Katherine is driven away by Curly (whom Gittes had earlier hired to take both women to Ensenada in his boat) as Gittes and Evelyn prevent Cross from following her. As Evelyn drives off to follow her daughter, she is shot and killed much as in the film. At the end Gittes is led away by his fellow operatives, Walsh and Duffy, while Noah Cross kneels "on the ground, holding Evelyn's body, crying." This ending, while not cheerful, does at least indicate that the efforts of Gittes and Evelyn were not in vain; the innocent Katherine does escape from the evil influence of her conscienceless father/grandfather, who is also shown expressing grief (and possibly even remorse) over his daughter's body. At least some human values are affirmed in this ending.

In Polanski's ending, however, Katherine is left firmly within the grasp of Noah who may look upon his dead daughter with a measure of shock as he backs away from the car, but certainly does not shed any tears for her. As she is pulled away, Katherine is screaming, "No, no!"—her protest against her mother's death but also an appropriate response to the sort of future one might envisage her having with Noah. The prime source of evil in the film has gotten his way here just as he has with the water policy of Los Angeles. This scene also includes a final line from Jake Gittes that wasn't present in Towne's third draft. There, Gittes's concluding words were his last vigorous denunciation of Noah Cross: "Get him away from her [Evelyn's body]. He's responsible for everything! Get him away from her!" In the film itself, Jake only mutters the phrase, "as little as possible." The implications of this utterance need to be considered.

When he was a police officer in Chinatown Jake was advised by the district attorney to do "as little as possible," but he apparently tried to do more than that, in an effort to "keep someone from being hurt"—with the result that he made "sure she was hurt." Now his efforts to save Evelyn and Katherine have led only to Evelyn's death and Katherine's possession by Noah Cross. Seeing once again a negative outcome to his striving to do good, Gittes repeats the phrase "as little as possible" as if acknowledging the wisdom of the D.A.'s advice and proclaiming the futility of all struggle against the forces of destruction. On the other hand, if one examines Gittes's behavior in the final sequences of the film, one might reach the conclusion he has done *almost* "as little as possible" to aid Evelyn and Katherine. Whereas in Towne's third draft, Gittes fought vigorously with Cross and Mulvihill to make time for Katherine to escape with Curly (141), in the film the detective does little more than stand by handcuffed to a policeman while the burden of defending herself and her sister/daughter is borne almost entirely by Evelyn. *She* is the one who might have been better off doing as little as possible.

Although most viewers of the film probably find him attractive, J. J. Gittes in the last analysis is a hollow man—the mere semblance of the hard-boiled private eye, not the real thing. This detective is a specialist in appearances. Through the first half of the film, Gittes wears a different, immaculately pressed suit in almost every sequence—even when the new sequence would seem most likely to be taking place the same day as the previous one. Production designer Anthea Sylbert apparently conceived of Gittes as a man who modeled his wardrobe on the apparel of the Hollywood leading men of the 1930s: "his clothing, she thought, would reflect 'an outsider's idea of how a star would dress'" (Leaming 142). When Evelyn Mulwray is leaving the morgue after identifying her husband's body, Gittes hustles her past a waiting group of reporters and cameramen, then turns in the doorway and poses himself—flashing a big star smile. The slashed nose and the unsightly bandage Gittes is forced to wear for much of the remainder of the film are not only reminders of his impotence but also signs of how vulnerable his self-created star image is.

Neither Polanski nor the audience can blame Gittes for his failure to protect Evelyn and Katherine at the end of the film. The death of Evelyn is technically an accident: A warning shot by the policeman Loach happened to hit her in the back of the head, with the exit wound through her eye. But because of the heavy symbolic foreshadowing of this event, it doesn't feel like an accident. R. Barton Palmer mentions some of the images that prepare for the final catastrophe: "Cross's glasses . . . found with one lens shattered, the one tail light on Mrs. Mulwray's car which Gittes breaks . . ., and, most importantly, the imperfection in Mrs. Mulwray's eye" (117). To these may be added the black eye of Curly's wife, a consequence of Gittes's previous investigation and a foreshadowing of a slightly different nature: Evelyn's involuntary sounding of her car's horn when she puts her head down on the steering wheel the night Gittes finds her with her "sister" presages the long wail of the horn when her dead body slumps against the wheel. With all of these portents, Evelyn Mulwray seems the victim less of chance than of an inexorable fate.

For Polanski, Evelyn's death is indeed unavoidable, for it is the echo or reflection not only of a prior disaster experienced by Jake Gittes but also of two terrible losses in the director's own life. *Chinatown* was released in 1974; five years earlier, Polanski's pregnant young wife, the actress Sharon Tate, was brutally slain by followers of Charles Manson. Certainly, the "sense of outrage" Polanski wanted to create with Evelyn's death in the film must have reflected his own feelings about his wife's murder; but Polanski's autobiography strongly suggests that the character of Evelyn more directly represents another woman in his life. Polanski says that he selected Faye Dunaway for the part "on the ground that her special brand of 'retro' beauty—the same sort of look I remembered in my mother—was essential to the film" (350). Earlier in the book he describes his mother's appearance: "I recall . . . her elegance, the precise way she drew the lines over her plucked eyebrows" (14-15). Those same precise lines appear over Evelyn's plucked brows in *Chinatown*. Polanski's mother was picked up by the Nazis during their occupation of Poland; years later he learned "that she had died in a gas chamber only days after being taken away" (58). It is not surprising that J. J. Gittes appears powerless to rescue Evelyn Mulwray when the director of the film could do nothing to save either mother or wife. Evelyn's death is an echo not only of J. J. Gittes's past but of Polanski's as well.

REFERENCES

Cawelti, John G. "*Chinatown* and Generic Transformation in Recent American Films." In *Film Genre Reader*, edited by Barry Keith Grant. Austin: University of Texas Press, 1986.

Leaming, Barbara. *Polanski, A Biography: The Filmmaker as Voyeur*. New York: Simon and Schuster, 1981.

Palmer, R. Barton. "Chinatown and the Detective Story." *Literature/Film Quarterly* 5 (1977): 112-17.

Polanski, Roman. *Roman by Polanski*. New York: William Morrow, 1984.

Simon, John. *Reverse Angle: A Decade of American Films*. New York: Clarkson N. Potter, 1982.

Towne, Robert. *Chinatown* (third draft). Hollywood: Script City, n.d.

10

Miller's Crossing:
The Poetics of Dashiell Hammett

Katherine M. Restaino

Tough guys dream their dreams and what does it get them? Trouble, murder, vicious beatings, physical pain, and mental suffering. The tough guy or, to be more precise, the *noble* tough guy of the gangster novels and gangster movies, borrowed by the Coen Brothers, Joel and Ethan, comes right from the pages of Dashiell Hammett. Max Allan Collins, in his review of the Coens' film *Miller's Crossing*, noted that he'd feel more generous if the line "'Based on a novel by Dashiell Hammett' appeared somewhere in the credits" (51). Collins reads the film as a version of *The Glass Key* in a number of obvious ways. Similarly, Henry Sheehan noted in *The Hollywood Reporter* that the film is "a finely worked tribute to the hard-boiled school of Dashiell Hammett. In fact, it is a bit more than a tribute: though the novelist's name does not appear anywhere in the credits, the film's plot bears a strong though not identical resemblance to *The Glass Key*."

Actually the Coens do acknowledge their debt to Hammett in the press-kit materials for *Miller's Crossing* (1990), but the specific novel mentioned is *Red Harvest*, published in 1923, not *The Glass Key*, which came out in 1931, or either of its film versions, the 1935 Paramount film with George Raft and Edward Arnold or the better-known 1942 remake starring Alan Ladd, Brian Donlevy, and, of course, Veronica Lake. As the Coens explained it, they wanted to do a gangster movie, not another *Raising Arizona*. The image Ethan Coen (co-screenwriter and producer) used as the kernel for the movie was one of "Big guys in overcoats in the woods—the incongruity of urban gangsters in a forest setting," an image more poetic in setting but similar in concept to the burial grounds for rubouts years ago—the Jersey meadowlands and the flatlands of Canarsie. The urban swamps were rural and odoriferous; the woods of *Miller's Crossing* are majestic and cathedral-like, an idyllic setting contaminated by death and the smells of death. Tom Reagan (Gabriel Byrne) vomits because of his certainty that he will die when Eddie Dane (J. E. Freeman) discovers that Tom didn't kill Bernie Bernbaum, a wonderful portrait of a creep played by John Turturro. Shortly after, Johnny Caspar's men discover a rotting, faceless corpse, later identified as the body of Mink Larouie (Steven Buscemi), not Bernie Bernbaum. As he also explains in the press kit, Joel Coen (co-screen-writer and director) wanted to make a movie inspired by novels, and Dashiell Hammett was a natural source because "he took the genre and used it to tell a story that was interesting about people and other things besides just the plot. In Hammett the plot is like a big jigsaw puzzle that can be seen in the background. It may make some internal sense, but the momentum of the characters is more important."

Hammett's *Red Harvest* and *The Glass Key* and their spin-off, *Miller's Crossing*, share common motifs and characteristics of the gangster genre. All three are stories of political corruption set in small cities. In each, a political boss has an advisor who is smarter and more perceptive than he. In *The Glass Key*, Paul Madvig, a small-time politician on the take, depends on Ned Beaumont for everything, including advice on matters of love and what socks to wear. Beaumont's counterpart in *Miller's Crossing* is Tom Reagan, whose suggestions go unheeded by Leo Duchaime (Albert Finney). The parallel in *Red Harvest* is not exact because the hero is not a political advisor and buddy but the Continental Op himself, who is hired from the outside by Donald Willson, publisher of the town newspaper. Willson wants the Op to eliminate the corruption from the town of Personville, Montana, better known as Poisonville. When Donald is killed, his elderly father, Elihu, who helped bring political corruption to Poisonville, retains the Op to solve the murder. Once the murderer is discovered, Elihu wants the Op to leave, but as matter of conscience, the Op cannot because the poison is still in Poisonville.

Beaumont, Reagan, and the Op are all men of principle, noble tough guys, operating in a world outside of the law, walking a lonely road, because they are truly solitary. Despite their value as advisors, Beaumont and Reagan do not get close to people, and they reject help from others with regard to personal matters. Ned Beaumont's description of himself "as a gambler and a politician's hanger-on" (Hammett 142) applies equally to Tom Reagan. Both men owe money to their bookies: Horse races and cards are not always their wisest pursuits. Both refuse to let their bosses pay their gambling debts. As a matter of honor, they take responsibility for their bad bets and will pay up themselves or take the consequences. Both men are beaten up for failing to pay off. Right after Tom is beaten, one of Lazarre's enforcers says to Tom: "It's nothing personal. Lazarre told us not to break anything, but he can't let people think he's soft."

The code of ethics is as strong in *Miller's Crossing* as in *The Glass Key*. Ethically, men don't welch on gambling debts; they remain loyal to the bosses; they follow the rules. *Miller's Crossing* opens with Johnny Caspar's (Jon Polito) discourse on ethics: Ethics, he tells Leo and Tom, "is the grease [that] makes us get along, what separates us from the animals, beasts o' burden, beasts o' prey, Ethics." Johnny is upset because Bernie Bernbaum places bets based on tips about the fights Johnny has been fixing. Leo, who receives protection money from Johnny Caspar, refuses Johnny's request to rub out Bernie Bernbaum because Leo's girl is Verna, Bernie's sister. Tom advises Leo that his denial of Johnny's request is a violation of the rules, a "bad play," especially since Johnny Caspar pays for protection.

A strong parallel to this incident occurs in *The Glass Key*. Paul Madvig refuses to spring Walt Ivan's brother Tim from jail until after the election. Ned Beaumont advises Paul Madvig to follow the rules—it's not worth the war that will occur because of his alliance with Senator Ralph Henry and Paul's infatuatition with Janet Henry, the senator's daughter. When Madvig refuses to hear Shad O'Rory's request to take care of the Ivans, O'Rory says "Business is business and politics is politics. Let's keep them apart" (65). Madvig and Leo continue to confuse the two. They reject the advice of their counselors because of their feelings for a woman, thus endangering their power and even their own lives.

In his speech on ethics, Johnny Caspar focuses on three qualities: "friendship, character, ethics," qualities that characterize Tom Reagan and Ned Beaumont. Both men display remarkable ingenuity and fortitude in maintaining these qualities and loyalty to their bosses, although ironically, while they protect them at peril to their own lives, they will not remain friends and advisors once the immediate problems have been resolved. Their bosses have overstepped the boundaries and have violated the accepted ethical codes of their rotten, corrupt worlds. Ned Beaumont's declaration, "I can stand anything I've got to stand" (5) is the raison d'être of his character and of Reagan's. Similarly, Tom Reagan tells Leo that he can take anything he has to take.

The Continental Op, Ned Beaumont, and Tom Reagan are simultaneously detached and yet very much involved in the action. They confide in no one as they move inexorably in a direction that puts them in grave danger yet saves their bosses. Their aloofness and their intelligence lead to a restoration of order, but in their triumph they resort to much that is on the fringe of the law. Ned Beaumont and Tom Reagan institute double crosses and double-double crosses to achieve their ends, and perhaps these are more complicated in *Miller's Crossing*. Tom deliberately breaks with Leo by telling him that Verna has slept with Tom, then goes to Johnny Caspar's camp where an immediate goal is to cause divisiveness between the Dane and Mink Larouie in order to make Johnny Caspar doubt the Dane's loyalty. Tom thinks nothing of double-crossing Caspar by not killing Bernie Bernbaum, who then tries to blackmail Tom (the thanks he gets for saving the creep's life). Once Tom has succeeded in turning Caspar against the Dane, all the ends are neatly wrapped up as Tom sets up Johnny Caspar to be killed by Bernie Bernbaum. When Tom ignores Bernie's usual plea for mercy ("Look in your heart"), Tom replies, "What heart?" and kills him.

The job that had to be done—the protection of Leo—is finished. Tom is alone. Verna has rejected him for Leo, and Tom leaves Leo because nothing can be the same.

Tom Reagan's solitary nature is emphasized in many ways in *Miller's Crossing*. He is always the man on the outside controlling the action inside—but a man who belongs nowhere, no longer part of Leo's gang and not really allied with Johnny Caspar. Moreover, images of solitude reoccur throughout the film: scenes of Tom alone in his semicircular room; long shots of Leo's office where the distance between Leo's desk and where Tom usually stands seems enormous and slightly off-center; the long shot of Tom against the tree in the cemetery. The aloofness of Tom Reagan's character is also represented in many ways by the image of the hat. When the film opens, the audience sees a hat being buffeted by the winds at Miller's Crossing. When Tom loses his hat in a card game and Verna gets it, he goes in search of it and gets more. At one point, he has a dream that he describes to Verna:

Tom: I was walking in the woods, don't know why. . . . The wind came up and blew my hat off. . . .

Verna: And you chased it, right? You ran and ran and finally you caught up to it and picked it up but it wasn't a hat anymore. It has changed into something else—something wonderful.

Tom: No. It stayed a hat. And no I didn't chase it. I watched it blow away. . . . Nothing more foolish than a man chasing his hat.

The way Tom wears his hat throughout the movie demonstrates his vulnerability to Verna, his style, his independence, and his distance. In the closing scene, borrowed from the film *The Third Man*, as he leans against the tree watching Leo walk away from the cemetery, he deliberately adjusts his fedora so that it appears to cover his eyes and shadow his face, as if to say, "I have my hat back and myself—and no one can get close to me again." It is his silent but telling declaration of independence.

Much of the action in *Miller's Crossing* is the result of Tom's search for his hat. When Gabriel Byrne asked Joel Coen about the importance of Tom's hat, Joel's response was simply, "The hat is very significant."[1] In *The Glass Key* hats were also important to the plot resolution. When Taylor Henry was murdered, his hat was not by his body, yet he had been wearing a hat when he left the house. When Ned Beaumont tries to find the murderer, he deliberately leaves one of Taylor's hats in the hotel suite of Bernie Despain, a bookie, not to frame Bernie but to exert pressure so that Bernie will provide some much-needed information. The Coens use the idea of the hat to move the action, specifically to bring Tom and Verna together, but it is possible that the Coens were capitalizing on the Irish tradition of the importance of a man's hat as a symbol of esteem, good standing, and personal ownership. One Irish ditty contains the lines: "I had a hat when I came in, and I put it on the rack;/I'll have a hat when I go out, or I'll break somebody's back."[2] Also, Johnny Patterson's song "The Hat My Father Wore" alludes to the connection between a hat's generational descent over many years and the honor of an Irish heritage (Thornton 92).

The dream motif, of course, comes from *The Glass Key*. Janet Henry dreams that she and Ned Beaumont reach a house with a glass key in the door. Through the window they see food, and as they are both hungry, they want to eat, but the floor is filled with snakes. If Janet and Ned open the door to get the food, the key will break and they will be attacked by the snakes. When Janet first recounts the dream, she tells Ned that they got the food and avoided the snakes. As Will Murray points out in "The Riddle of *The Glass Key*" there are many interpretations attached to the dream: bad luck, guilt, sexuality, the dangers of knowledge (290-93). It is possible that the glass key has oversymbolized, that the title of the novel was just that—a title Hammett got from a friend—before he ever finished writing the installments of the novel for the magazine *Black Mask*.

Red Harvest also exploits the narrative function of dreams. First, the Op dreams of a search for a veiled woman who, when he finds her, kisses him in front of everyone. The people watching them start to laugh. In another dream, the Op chases a man to the roof, grabs him, but falls off with him. William Marling, in his critical study of Hammett, describes the dreams as functional bridges to action: The dream of the veiled woman is a symbolic version of Dinah Brand's death. The second dream is a reminder that emotion leads to death (54).

The violence of the gangster novel becomes especially evident, perhaps even best described as choreographed, in the gangster movie. *Red Harvest*, for example, ends up with more than two dozen deaths, and this influence carries over to *Miller's Crossing*. The Op is the recipient of some very rough and brutal beatings, as is Ned Beaumont, whose working over by Shad O'Rory's thugs in *The Glass Key* is one of the most graphic ever described in a novel. It was equally graphic in the 1942 film, where one wonders if Alan Ladd (called Ed Beaumont) will survive; and Tom Reagan receives even more beatings in a relatively short period of time in *Miller's Crossing*. The sequence begins Tom's repudiation by Leo, who pursues him through the second-floor corridor and down the stairs to the public rooms of the Shenandoah Club. Later Johnny Caspar's henchman beats Tom in the warehouse-like atmosphere of Caspar's Club. As Tom leaves a phone booth, he gets it in the gut from one of Leo's men. Finally, there's the "friendly" but necessary beating by Lazarre's men as a warning to Tom to pay his gambling debts. The Coens capture the brutality in rhythms appropriate to the action: The beating in the Shenandoah Club lasts the longest and uses more space because it is a demonstration of public repudiation and betrayal. Although the beatings may represent nothing more than a warning in some cases or a punishment in others, as each one occurs the physical space becomes more confined because the issue at hand is more limited.

One choreographed scene of violence, the famous machine-gun battle, seems a gloss on the gangster film's formula of violence.[3] As Leo sits in bed, smoking a cigar and listening to a Frank Patterson recording of "Danny Boy," he becomes aware of smoke drifting up from the floorboards of his bedroom. Assuming that there are intruders in the house, Leo carefully stubs out the cigar, puts it in the pocket of his silk dressing gown, grabs his gun, gets on the floor under the bed, and makes mincemeat of his assailants. The scene is punctuated by what appears to be a thousand rounds of ammunition and a crescendo of music. Leo climbs out the window, shimmies down the drainpipe, and starts firing at the getaway car, which careens down the driveway and blows up. Leo takes out his cigar and relights it, ending a careful, deliberate scene of violence—an old-fashioned gangster fight recreated in a highly stylized format. Geoff Andrews selected this scene as the film's most memorable moment; the scene should be viewed as one that makes *Miller's Crossing* what the Coens refer to in the press kit as a "genre movie."

The love angle in *Miller's Crossing* is very much reminiscent of Hammett's portrayal of women and use of women to advance the plots of both *Red Harvest* and the *The Glass Key*. In his review of *Miller's Crossing* in *The Nation*, Stuart Klawans suggests that the film would be better if there were "a stronger female character, or two or three." This observation goes against the grain of Hammett's gangster novels, where the stories are men's stories in which one female character (or two at the most) is essential as a means of providing complications to the plot. Even though two women figure in *Red Harvest* (Dinah Brand and Mrs. Donald Willson) and *The Glass Key* (Janet Henry and Opal Madvig), Dinah and Janet are the only significant ones. The Op, while recognizing Dinah's philosophy of life that there is no such thing as a favor or free information, still makes some careless moves because of his fascination with her. Both Paul Madvig and Ned Beaumont allow themselves to become entangled in dangerous situations because of Janet Henry's glamour and intrigue. Although Ned cautions Paul about letting his feelings for Janet interfere with his business and political decisions, Ned falls into the same trap.

In *Miller's Crossing* Verna is an amalgam of Dinah Brand and Janet Henry. Like Hammett's women, Verna does what is necessary to protect her brother Bernie Bernbaum by becoming Leo's girl, but Verna does not have Janet Henry's style, good looks, or sophistication. If anything, she could be Dinah Brand's sister. Verna never really looks attractive in *Miller's Crossing*. Although she's not messy and unkempt the way Dinah Brand is (Dinah wears dresses ripped at the seams, stockings with runs in them, streaked makeup), Verna must have some appeal for men, probably "bed artistry," to quote her brother. Dinah Brand sells information; she never gives anything away. Janet Henry, on the other hand, will buy information and protection in order to save both her brother and father. All three women, in different ways, do what is necessary to achieve their ends.

The Coen Brothers created a novel as screenplay in *Miller's Crossing*. The spare, lean language and objectivity of Hammett's *Red Harvest* and *The Glass Key* served as models for an evocation of an order, an era, and a style where friendship and loyalty are called upon to end chaos and upheaval. In *Red Harvest* there is a restoration of order, in *Miller's Crossing* and *The Glass Key* a restoration to the "orderly" state of political corruption. Paul Madvig and Leo Duchaime have each lost a counselor. Both men may have learned a slight lesson about what happens when one ruptures the order of doing things, but they have not learned the real lesson. In breaking the rules, they lost the trust of their counselors, who, even on the shady side of the law, have deeply ingrained principles of friendship, character, and ethics.

Throughout *Miller's Crossing* Tom frequently exhorts Leo to think—to think about his obligation to Johnny Caspar as a businessman who is paying for protection; to think about his weakness for Verna and how it will topple his control of the city; to think of how people will interpret his lack of resolve as a sign of vulnerability. Johnny Caspar constantly prefaces sentences with "I think," as does the Dane. Ironically, after Rug Daniels is killed, there is thought given to figure out why Rug's hairpiece was taken; in a symbolic but effective scene a little boy and his dog find a corpse, and the youngster, fascinated by the sight of a dead man sitting against a wall, removes the hairpiece as a memento of an unusual sight. Tom constantly weighs thought and action. His thought leads to action and back to thought. At the film's conclusion, the camera tracks away from the image of Tom leaning against the tree, and the dream of the man chasing his hat becomes understood as the pursuit of self-knowledge. "Nothing more foolish than a man chasing his hat" were Tom's own words about the dream; but when Tom so carefully puts on his hat and adjusts the brim downward, he has finished this phase of his life, because he reaffirms who and what he is. The woods of *Miller's Crossing* have indeed revealed the landscape of the mind.

NOTES

1. See Mark Horowitz, "Coen Brothers A-Z: The Big Two-Headed Picture." Also, Tom Shone, "Cult Movie Making by Numbers."

2. This was suggested to me by W. Russel Gray, professor of English, Delaware County Community College.

3. Merrill Shindler describes this scene as "one of the greatest machinegun fight scenes of all time. By comparison, the battles in *Dick Tracy* are wimpy. *Miller's Crossing* separates the men from the simply boyish."

REFERENCES

Andrews, Geoff. "The Coen Brothers and 'Barton Fink.'" *Time Out*, February 15, 1992.
Collins, Max Allan. "Mystery Seen." *Mystery Scene* 28 (January 1991).
Hammett, Dashiell. *The Glass Key*. New York: Vintage Books/Random House, 1972.

Horowitz, Mark. "Coen Brothers A-Z: The Big Two-Headed Picture." *Film Comment*, 27, no. 5 (September-October 1991): 28-29.

Klawans, Stuart. "Films." *The Nation*, November 5, 1990, 537-40.

Marling, William. *Dashiell Hammett*. Boston: Twayne, 1983.

Miller's Crossing press kit. Twentieth Century Fox. 1990.

Murray, Will. "The Riddle of *The Glass Key*." *Armchair Detective* 3, no. 22 (Summer 1989): 290-93.

Sheehan, Henry. *Hollywood Reporter*, August 20, 1990. From *Miller's Crossing* clippings file. Margaret Herrick Library. Center for Motion Picture Study, Los Angeles, CA.

Shindler, Merrill. *Los Angeles Magazine*, September 1990. From *Miller's Crossing* clippings file. Margaret Herrick Library. Center for Motion Picture Study, Los Angeles, CA.

Shone, Tom. "Cult Movie Making by Numbers." *London Sunday Times*, cinema section, February 9, 1992, 6.

Thornton, Weldon. *Allusions in Ulysses*. Chapel Hill: University of North Carolina Press, 1968.

11

The "Very Simplicity of the Thing": Edgar Allan Poe and the Murders He Wrote

Jan Whitt

Edgar Allan Poe (1809-1849) left the world a collection of poems, essays, tales of terror, and detective fiction, all dedicated to the belief that art must appeal both to reason and to emotion. It is in his three detective stories, however, that Poe best defends the interdependence of logic and intuition in reaching what he unabashedly calls "truth." In "Sonnet to Science," a poem Poe wrote when he was twenty, he reveals an early cynicism about the ascendancy of technological development:

> Science! true daughter of Old Time thou art!
>   Who alterest all things with thy peering eyes.
> Why preyest thou thus upon the poet's heart,
>   Vulture, whose wings are dull realities?
> How should he love thee? or how deem thee wise?
>   Who wouldst not leave him in his wandering
> To seek for treasure in the jewelled skies,
>   Albeit he soared with an undaunted wing?
> Has thou not dragged Diana from her car?
>   And driven the Hamadryad from the wood
> To seek a shelter in some happier star?
>   Has thou not torn the Naiad from her flood,
> The Elfin from the green grass, and from me
> The summer dream beneath the tamarind tree? (788)

The disciple of Samuel Taylor Coleridge (1772-1834) and the contemporary of Nathaniel Hawthorne (1804-1864), Poe was part of a worthy tradition that suspected Science of draining the life and emotion from art by trying to eradicate mystery from the earth (Poe therefore accuses Science of dragging Diana from her "car"—the moon—symbol of mystery or inconstancy).

Matthew Arnold (1822-1888), also a contemporary of Poe's, espoused a fear of excessive rationality adopted at the expense of faith and poetry in the modern world. In his famous essay "The Study of Poetry," Arnold wrote of poetry as a force that would complete the role of science in transforming the earth:

More and more mankind will discover that we have to turn to poetry to interpret life for us, to console us, to sustain us. Without poetry, our science will appear incomplete; and most of what now passes with us for religion and philosophy will be replaced by poetry. Science, I say, will appear incomplete without it. (306)

Arnold also noted the importance of "regularity, uniformity, precision, [and] balance" in writing and in decisions, but he warned against the "exclusive attention to these qualities" because of the "repression and silencing of poetry" (321) that might result. Poetry, obviously, meant more to Arnold than verse; for him it was a power capable of unifying humankind, as he believed religion once had done.

Although Poe might have been especially devoted to Coleridge and connected philosophically to Arnold, one also must recognize his link to at least one of his contemporaries in America, Hawthorne. Certainly, the spirit of the times in both Britain and America involved a reverence for science and a fear that humankind had lost its spiritual center. In a series of short stories and novels reminiscent of *Frankenstein* (1817) by Mary Wollstonecraft Shelley (1797-1851), Hawthorne analyzes the role of the scientist and physician too devoted to factual analysis. The theme runs through "Rappaccini's Daughter," "The Birthmark," *The Scarlet Letter*, and other works and testifies to Hawthorne's fear of the possibilities of a mind separated from the heart. The most damning description of the man of science occurs in the first paragraph of "The Birthmark":

In the latter part of the last century there lived a man of science, an eminent proficient in every branch of natural philosophy, who not long before our story opens had made experience of a spiritual affinity more attractive than any chemical one. He had . . . persuaded a beautiful woman to become his wife. In those days when the comparatively recent discovery of electricity and other kindred mysteries of Nature seemed to open paths into the region of miracle, it was not unusual for the love of science to rival the love of woman in its depth and absorbing energy. (707)

At the end of the tale, the man devoted "too unreservedly to scientific studies" kills his wife while attempting to remove a blemish from her face in a vain search for perfection and for a symbol of "man's ultimate control over Nature" (707).

Poe proposes later in his career that the analytical perspective of mathematics and the physical sciences is limited, and in C. Auguste Dupin he unites the critical powers of reasoning and the perception and energy of the heart. Like Coleridge and William Wordsworth (1770-1850), Poe struggled not to treat scientific discovery as arrogant bluff but to balance it with the longings of the human spirit. Coleridge writes in Chapter 1 of *Biographia Literaria* that while he was a student, he learned that "poetry, even that of the loftiest and, seemingly, that of the wildest odes, had a logic of its own as severe as that of science; and more difficult, because more subtle, more complex, and dependent on more, and more fugitive, causes" (341). In Chapter 4, he pays tribute to the "union of deep feeling with profound thought" (349), as does Wordsworth in the "Preface to the *Lyrical Ballads*":

The knowledge both of the poet and the man of science is pleasure; but the knowledge of the one cleaves to us as a necessary part of our existence, our natural and unalienable inheritance; the other is a personal and individual acquisition, slow to come to us, and by no habitual and direct sympathy connecting us with our fellow-beings. The man of science seeks truth as a remote and unknown benefactor; he cherishes and loves it in his solitude: the poet, singing a song in which all human beings join with him, rejoices in the presence of truth as our visible friend and hourly companion. Poetry is the breath and finer spirit of all knowledge; it is the impassioned expression which is in the countenance of all science. . . . Poetry is the first and last of all knowledge—it is as immortal as the heart of man. (136)

Poe remained in sympathy with Coleridge and Wordsworth as he wrote "The Purloined Letter," "The Murders in the Rue Morgue," and "The Mystery of Marie Roget (A Sequel to 'The Murders in the Rue Morgue')." He leaves the cerebral Parisian police acting from habit and past experience, while his famous detective solves the cases as much through an understanding of the human spirit as through a detached analysis of data.

The influence of Poe's detective fiction on American mystery writers has been well documented, but the relationship between Dupin and the detectives of popular culture depicted in a television series such as *Columbo* or *Murder, She Wrote* is not as extensive. An examination of *Murder, She Wrote* reveals several important similarities between the philosophy behind Poe's three short stories and the formula that drives the creators of *Murder, She Wrote*. Most important, the study identifies the central concern of Dupin and Jessica Fletcher: never to miss what Poe terms the "very simplicity of the thing" ("The Purloined Letter" 918) in the midst of the complexities of the case. Other similarities prove the point:

1) each detective, although involved in an occupation that requires solitude, discusses every case with a a close friend, thereby allowing the reader/viewer to keep pace with the discoveries;

2) each detective compiles data after sorting through the accounts of multiple witnesses replete with details, irrelevant observations, and misleading signifiers;

3) each detective is treated as if he/she were a bungler

who—in spite of an established reputation—must earn
the respect of the law enforcement officials he/she
seeks to help; and

4) each detective attests repeatedly to his or her astute
reading of people, who are the subtexts in the phenomenological nightmare of crimes and murders.

THE METHODS OF C. AUGUSTE DUPIN

In one of Poe's most popular stories, "The Purloined Letter," the narrator
discusses the two previous cases which his friend Dupin solved, "The Murders
in the Rue Morgue" and "The Mystery of Marie Roget." A visit by the Prefect
of the Parisian police activates the plot, as Dupin is immediately set up as
superior to his guest. The narrator explains that the Prefect has the unfortunate
habit of ridiculing what he cannot understand. The Prefect, he says, "had a
fashion of calling every thing 'odd' that was beyond his comprehension, and
thus lived amid an absolute legion of 'oddities.'" These oddities create for the
Prefect an impenetrable jungle in which he struggles and fails to make sense of
the sign system. Coming to Dupin for help in recovering a stolen letter, the
Prefect admits to his failure without understanding that the cause is his lack of
self-perception:

"The fact is, we have all been a good deal puzzled because the affair *is* so simple, and
yet baffles us altogether." "Perhaps it is the very simplicity of the thing which puts you
at fault," said my friend. "What nonsense you *do* talk!" replied the Prefect, laughing
heartily. "Perhaps the mystery is a little *too* plain," said Dupin. "Oh, good heavens!
who ever heard of such an idea?" "A little *too* self-evident." "Ha! ha! ha!—ha! ha!
ha!—ho! ho! ho!" roared out our visitor, profoundly amused, "oh, Dupin, you will be
the death of me yet!" (918)

Poe reveals the Prefect's weakness through short sections of dramatic
monologue, in which the official reveals more about himself than he intends.
Discussing the man who took a letter that contains secrets dangerous to a high-
ranking government official, the Prefect assesses his opponent by saying, "Not
altogether a fool, but then he's a poet, which I take to be only one remove from
a fool." The reader thereby understands that the Prefect operates with only half
of his capacities; the reader then may choose to identify with Dupin, who
confesses in an ironically self-deprecating way that he himself is "guilty of
certain doggerel" (921).

The Prefect and the Parisian police searched the thief's apartment for the
letter and are now at a loss, although they are certain they have the right man.
To the narrator, Dupin explains that the measures the Prefect used "were good
in their kind and well executed; their defect lay in their being inapplicable to the
case, and to the man" (925).

A certain set of highly ingenious resources are, with the Prefect, a sort of Procrustean bed, to which he forcibly adapts his designs. But he perpetually errs by being too deep or too shallow, for the matter in hand; and many a schoolboy is a better reasoner than he. (925)

Dupin then tells his friend two parables, the first involving a young boy who wins consistently in a game of marbles. The boy reads the faces of his opponents, reasons, observes, trusts experience—and wins, a feat that his acquaintances attribute to luck. Lacking these abilities, the Prefect is crippled, Dupin suggests. He implicates the Prefect when he describes a group of people who operate from custom alone:

They consider only their *own* ideas of ingenuity; and, in searching for anything hidden, advert only to the modes in which *they* would have hidden it. They are right in this much—that their own ingenuity is a faithful representative of that of *the mass*; but when the cunning of the individual felon is diverse in character from their own, the felon foils them, of course. This always happens when it is above their own, and very usually, when it is below. They have no variation of principle in their investigations; at best, when urged by some unusual emergency—by some extraordinary reward—they extend or exaggerate their old modes of *practice*, without touching their principles. (926)

In a second parable later in "The Purloined Letter," Dupin describes what he calls "a game of puzzles which is played upon a map." In this game, "overlarge-ly lettered signs and placards of the street" escape "observation by dint of being excessively obvious" (929). Through both short narratives, Dupin makes clear to his listener the failure of the Prefect to investigate the nature of the man he seeks to trap, an investigation that is at root a poetic enterprise.

In "The Purloined Letter," Dupin eventually combines the quantitative skills of the mathematician (respected in the culture) with the qualitative powers of the poet (assumed to be the fool) and finds the stolen letter in the Minister's apartment. The limitations of the mathematical approach are revealed when Dupin says:

There are numerous other mathematical truths which are only truths within the limits of *relation*. But the mathematician argues, from his *finite truths*, through habit, as if they were of an absolutely general applicability—as the world indeed imagines them to be. (927-928)

By opening scientific premises to the scrutiny of the poetic mind, Dupin testifies to the importance of the two powers working in tandem. By practicing what he preaches, Dupin at last seeks a rack with "five or six visiting cards and a solitary letter" in the Minister's home. "This last was much soiled and crumpled," Poe writes of the letter. "It was torn nearly in two, across the middle—as if a design, in the first instance, to tear it entirely up as worthless, had been altered, or stayed, in the second" (930). The detective finds the letter because he knows the Parisian police have checked every hidden corner on the premises; he deduces that the letter must be in plain sight. In the end he spots the letter by realizing that a soiled and torn letter is antithetical to the Minister's own character, since he is by nature compulsively clean and organized: "The *radicalness* of these differences, which was excessive, the dirt; the soiled and torn condition of the paper, so inconsistent with the *true* methodical habits" (930) of the Minister alerted Dupin. Not only does Dupin gain the 50,000 francs offered by the Prefect for helping to solve the case, but he gains the respect of the police force and the pleasure of having outsmarted the Minister, to whom he sends a personal message by replacing the letter he has retrieved with a letter resembling it.

In "The Murders in the Rue Morgue," Poe holds consistently to the motivating philosophy of his earlier two detective sagas. Once again, the necessity of the analytical mind working with intuition is established early. The world, says Dupin, believes that "the calculating and discriminating powers (causality and comparison) are at variance with the imaginative—that the three, in short, can hardly coexist" (655). However, Dupin says:

[Although] thus opposed to received opinion, the idea will not appear ill-founded when we observe that the processes of invention or creation are strictly akin with the processes of resolution—the former being nearly, if not absolutely, the latter conversed. (655)

Quite simply, Dupin argues, the results "brought about by the very soul and essence of method, have, in truth, the whole air of intuition" (656). The gift of the poet, Dupin believes, is the ability to "observe attentively" and thereby to "remember distinctly" (657).

Using these powers, Dupin finds the unlikely killer of Madame L'Espanaye and her daughter, Mademoiselle Camille L'Espanaye: an "Ourang-Outang" from the East Indian Islands. The ape had been brought to Europe by a sailor, who lost the animal and disappeared after the crime, afraid of his own responsibility in the brutal deaths. Another man has been wrongly accused of the murders, and Dupin sets a trap to find the sailor, reassures him of his innocence if he testifies, and thereby frees the accused. "Murders in the Rue Morgue," which Dupin calls a "riddle," reinforces "The Purloined Letter" by implicating those who cannot see what is too obvious. Dupin said, "It appears to me that this mystery is considered insoluble, for the very reasons which should cause it to be regarded as easy of solution—I mean for the *outre* character of its features" (670). Criticizing a Frenchman for his shortsightedness, Dupin tells the narrator:

He impaired his vision by holding the object too close. He might see, perhaps, one or two points with unusual clearness, but in so doing he, necessarily, lost sight of the matter as a whole. Thus, there is such a thing as being too profound. Truth is not always in a well. (668)

For the semiologist who equates a detective and his/her clues with a reader exploring the signs of a text, "The Murders in the Rue Morgue" and "The Mystery of Marie Roget" are especially rich. In "The Murders in the Rue Morgue," data are accumulated through interviews with multiple witnesses who speak several languages—Italian, English, Spanish, French, and others. The linguistic labyrinth overwhelms the police, since descriptions conflict with one another and facts seem shadowed by the varied perceptions, some of which *must* be wrong. The differences in the languages themselves make even the cognates problematic, and the nuances and semantic puzzles testify to the basic unreliability of language itself.

In "The Mystery of Marie Roget," the same artistic effect is gained through the use of multiple newspaper stories in which selected facts are revealed. Dupin must solve both cases by gleaning information from accounts by witnesses and from published newspaper articles without being swayed and without missing the implications of those very accounts and stories. All three cases require that Dupin read varied texts (the Minister's apartment, the Minister himself, the Prefect, the police accounts of the crime, the newspaper stories, etc.).

In "The Mystery of Marie Roget," Mary Cecilia Rogers of New York is murdered, and her body is found floating in a river. The case remains unsolved, and Dupin has only newspaper accounts with which to work. Again, the central problem Dupin discovers in the coverage of others is their failure to reconcile the "most rigidly exact in science" (what he terms the "Calculus of Probabilities") with the "shadow and spirituality" of the "most intangible" (759) aspects of the case. Inverting his previous method in "The Purloined Letter" and "The Murders in the Rue Morgue," Dupin solves the crime, saying to the narrator:

I need scarcely tell you . . . that this is a far more intricate case than that of the Rue Morgue; from which it differs in one important respect. This is an *ordinary*, although an atrocious instance of crime. There is nothing peculiarly *outre* about it. You will observe that, for this reason, the mystery has been considered easy, when for this reason, it should have been considered difficult, of solution. (769)

Discovering that the murder was committed by a single person instead of a gang, as earlier believed, "the Chevalier's analytical abilities acquired for him the credit of intuition" (760), Poe writes. Dupin analyzes the nature of the gang and explains how the murder must have been committed by a single person who would have had to resort to dragging the body and leaving behind some of the evidence. He then analyzes the nature of the murderer himself, deduces his means of escape, and discusses his findings with the narrator. In all three stories, Dupin attests to the value of the scientific method wedded to the discernment of the human heart; to the value of close observation connected with an understanding of others; to the value of perseverance in the face of ridicule and doubt; and to the value of not remaining a slave to one's own favorite approach, an approach that may require modification during another case.

THE METHODS OF JESSICA B. FLETCHER

The first similarity between the detective in *Murder, She Wrote* and Dupin is the reliance of each on a friend or colleague with whom to discuss the facts of the case. Because both must reveal new discoveries that take place in an internal stream of consciousness, a narrator or friend standing in as listener is necessary organically. The reader/viewer must rely on spoken language as well as reconstructed scenes for understanding. In four episodes of *Murder, She Wrote*—all of which are representative of the series—Jessica B. Fletcher, played by Angela Lansbury, keeps the viewer up to date by talking to the local sheriff or doctor if she is in her hometown, Cabot Cove, Maine; or she relies on a relationship with an accused but ever-innocent person, a former friend, a new acquaintance, or the like if she is traveling before or during the commission of the crime.

Second, Jessica functions as a semiologist in the tradition of Dupin. While rarely wrestling with the stationary text of a witness's recorded account or a published newspaper story (as Dupin does), Fletcher often reconstructs the scene via speculation and reads the fluid texts—people—available to her. A physician who has been Fletcher's longtime friend in Cabot Cove tells a state health department official in "Keep the Home Fires Burning" that Fletcher is "the most observant person I know." In "Powder Keg," Fletcher, arguing against the guilt of an accused murderer during a conversation with the father of the dead man, Ed Bonner, attests to her ability to read those around her. She speaks in the following excerpt about Matthew Burns, accused of the murder:

Fletcher: But don't you think—I mean—if he's as much of a
          coward as you think he is, don't you think it's more
          likely he would have fired a gun from ambush?

Bonner: Are you an expert in killin'?

Fletcher: No. But I think I know something about people.

Unusually astute readings of those involved in the case make Jessica Fletcher a reliable translator of event.

The third similarity between Poe's creation of C. Auguste Dupin and the creation of Jessica Fletcher by Peter S. Fischer, Richard Levinson, and William Link is the necessity for the detectives to prove their worth to a skeptical person in power. Even when those in power are attacked by others and supported by the detective, their arrogance clouds their vision. For example, in "Powder Keg," a small Alabama community erupts when a town bully is killed at Kelso's, a local bar. The town sheriff, a black man, is besieged by residents who do not trust his handling of the case. One resident speaks the mind of the community when he calls the sheriff a "colored college boy." Andy Crane, a friend of the deceased, later adds, "All I see is a colored boy shakin' behind that badge." Even in this atmosphere, the sheriff is loath to accept the knowledge and support that Fletcher offers. In the other episodes, Fletcher must win over sheriffs, police, administrators, and others. Since the show is a series and not a serial, many of the characters change from week to week. With no time to characterize each participant in the case, the creators of *Murder, She Wrote* illustrate the importance of the characters through their function in the community; they are identified by their roles as waitresses, cooks, owners of diners, sheriffs, professors, or club owners, for example.

Just as Dupin is respected and praised only by the friend to whom he tells his story (since others associate him with being a magician but rarely praise his clearly superior observation skills), Fletcher must solve cases because of the pure joy she gains in doing so, not because she is paid or appreciated. When the plot evolves in Cabot Cove, Fletcher can expect support from longtime friends and the sheriff, played by Tom Bosley. But in "Keep the Home Fires Burning," a state health department official, Margot Perry, comes to Cabot Cove to investigate a death at the Joshua Peabody Inn on the outskirts of town. She has no role in solving the murder; in fact, she leaves the episode before the mur-derer is apprehended. Her work is complete when she understands that motive, not restaurant health standards, is at issue. Her reason for existing in the fictional world of the script is to challenge the courteous, mild-mannered authority of Jessica Fletcher. Fletcher's interest in the case is supported by friends because she too ate in the restaurant on the day of the death, but Perry continually ridicules her methods of investigation. To solve the cases in *Murder, She Wrote*, Fletcher often must discredit the person in control and wrest authority from him or her.

Occasionally, Fletcher is supported by what is perceived by the culture as the lower echelon of the community. In "Who Killed J. B. Fletcher?" a large portrait of Fletcher adorns the wall of a resident's home. The woman is a club member of the J. B. Fletcher Literary Society in a small town called Bremerton. When one of the residents assumes Jessica Fletcher's identity in order to solve a local mystery, she is killed as she inadvertently stumbles onto a murder. A headline in the *Bremerton Gazette* ("Mystery Writer Killed") alerts Fletcher that something is afoot. Going to the town to interview the friends of the murdered woman, Fletcher discovers the club formed in her honor. The homemakers who constitute its membership use their part-time positions and the reputations of their husbands to glean information for Fletcher. In finding the killer of their friend Marge Allen, they also uncover an insurance scam and the murder of a respected Bremerton resident. Proud of their achievement, the women hail Fletcher as their inspiration.

In every episode, Fletcher is the superintending narrator, the omniscient, perceptive humanist who not only brings order to the community she is in but also provides lessons about the value of compassion in dealing with one's fellows. In "Keep the Home Fires Burning," Fletcher notices that Harrison Fraser grieves more about the death of his friend than the illness of his wife after the two are poisoned while eating at the Joshua Peabody Inn. Fletcher eventually accuses his wife, Wilhemina, of murdering her lunch companion, a woman involved emotionally with Harrison Fraser. Wilhemina Fraser put poison in a jar of the restaurant's famous strawberry preserves, ate a small amount to make herself sick and remove herself from suspicion, and killed the woman. The jar is accidentally passed from table to table, and several other diners became ill. Fletcher reconstructs the scene, eliminates local residents and visitors from the list of suspects, and traps Wilhemina Fraser through an accurate reading of her character and the sorrow of her husband.

Jessica Fletcher never fails. When she befriends a character, that character will prove his or her worth and/or innocence in the end. When someone is rude to Fletcher or treats her with condescension, the viewer is assured that the person is worthless. In the universe of *Murder, She Wrote*, the predictable formula reassures the viewer of the possibility of order in a chaotic world and of the importance of emotion as a balance for the technical expertise involved in processing clues. Fletcher never misses the obvious or the hidden, and she constantly revises her strategy to avoid relying too heavily on previously effective methods. For example, in "Who Killed J. B. Fletcher?" when a prominent resident of Bremerton is killed, the police, led by Sheriff J. T. Tanner, are unable to ascertain the scene of the crime. Fletcher suggests that the murder occurred in the victim's own basement; she tells Tanner she believes the murderer stepped out from behind the stairs and shot the victim in the back as he walked toward a cabinet in the basement. Tanner, following the formula of the series, is hostile to Fletcher's ready analysis:

Tanner: Well, that's a tidy scenario, Mrs. Fletcher.
            Unfortunately, it's not backed up by any
            physical evidence.

Fletcher: Well, maybe we're overlooking something. I mean,
            something obvious—something in plain sight.

Fletcher finds the physical evidence—blood spattered on the basement lightbulb that is invisible when the light is on—and the sheriff acknowledges Fletcher as the better sleuth. Accused early in the episode of being too nosy, Fletcher admits, smiling, "It's a character flaw. I'm curious about everything." Fletcher is not only curious; she is accurate. When she announces that one of the suspects is not the right "type," the viewer can turn his or her attention elsewhere.

Fletcher, like Dupin, does not allow her analytical skills to overwhelm her instincts. She balances head with heart. Further, she never loses sight of the obvious, the "something in plain sight," that baffles the law enforcement officials involved in the case. Just as Dupin found the purloined letter by studying the character of the Minister carefully, Fletcher approaches the players in her cases as the complex signifying systems they are. Just as Dupin pays homage to the "very simplicity of the thing" in his investigations of the crime scene, Fletcher finds evidence others overlook as being too obvious. Both detectives must prove their worth to those in authority—much as Lieutenant Columbo also must do—and both are unaffected by the judgments of others. Finally, each shares with the audience his or her techniques via conversations with a friend or colleague, thereby increasing the pleasure of the reader or viewer by allowing familiarity and identification with that person. Edgar Allan Poe, master storyteller, provided the detective of Cabot Cove with a worthy predecessor indeed.

REFERENCES

Arnold, Matthew. "The Study of Poetry." In *Poetry and Criticism of Matthew Arnold*, edited by A. Dwight Culler. Boston: Houghton Mifflin, 1961.

Coleridge, Samuel Taylor. *Biographia Literaria*. In *The Norton Anthology of English Literature*, vol. 2, edited by M. H. Abrams et al. 3d ed. New York: W. W. Norton and Co., 1962.

Hawthorne, Nathaniel. "The Birthmark." In *The American Tradition in Literature*, vol. 1, edited by Sculley Bradley et al. 4th ed. New York: Grosset and Dunlap, 1974.

Poe, Edgar Allan. "The Murders in the Rue Morgue." In *The Unabridged Edgar Allan Poe*. Philadelphia: Running Press, 1983.

_____. "The Mystery of Marie Roget." In *The Unabridged Edgar Allan Poe*. Philadelphia: Running Press, 1983.

_____. "The Purloined Letter." In *The Unabridged Edgar Allan Poe*. Philadelphia: Running Press, 1983.

_____. "Sonnet-To Science." *The American Tradition in Literature*, vol. 1, edited by Sculley Bradley et al. 4th ed. New York: Grosset and Dunlap, 1974.

Wordsworth, William. "Preface to *Lyrical Ballads*." In *The Norton Anthology of English Literature*, vol. 2, edited by M. H. Abrams et al. 3d ed. New York: W. W. Norton and Co., 1962.

12

Done to Death?: Formula and Variation in *Perry Mason*

J. Dennis Bounds

Perry Mason, the successful lawyer-detective drama that aired in the 1950s and 1960s on CBS, was developed by a production company, Paisano Productions, owned by Erle Stanley Gardner. As the creator of the original *Perry Mason* mystery novels upon which the series was based, Gardner cared a great deal about the *Perry Mason* television series and its formula. A revealing instance illustrating the extent of Gardner's involvement in the weekly program occurred during preproduction work on "The Case of the Howling Dog." In a letter, Gardner railed at executive producer Gail Patrick Jackson because the scriptwriter, Seelig Lester, chose to use the barking-dog clue.

In this overused staple of mystery fiction, the detective identifies the murderer as someone familiar to the loyal family dog, rather than a stranger, because the dog doesn't bark when approached. Since Lester was adapting one of Gardner's original novels for this television episode, Gardner was furious that Lester changed what the author felt was a key plot point. In Gardner's novel, the prosecution tries to use this clue to convict Mason's client, and Mason is able to prove that the dog in fact had howled at the approach of the murderer and died defending the victim, thereby serving as a variation on the old clue (132-33). Gardner had originally varied the clue to disprove mystery writer "S. S. Van Dine's dictum that barking dogs serving as clues have been done to death." Gardner did not want any stale ideas in his series, yet Gardner resorted, book after book, episode after episode, to a formula that was quite recognizable. Audiences expected to see a similar program each week.

This essay uses two words extensively—*genre* and *formula*. Kaminsky and Mahan write that genre is order, and this order is neither "absolute" nor "exclusive." Genre becomes a "shared perspective" between critic and audience. As a tool for the critic, genre allows for an understanding of an episode or series by creating "a context for that understanding" (17-22). Formula, on the other hand, concerns their internal workings. Horace Newcomb considers *Perry Mason* to be emblematic of formulaic series television and goes on to define a successful formula as "a conventional system for structuring cultural products" (22). He stresses that any product's artistic merit should not be the focus of television analysis. It is not the purpose of this essay to argue artistic merits (or lack of them), but to examine the internal workings of *Perry Mason*, its formula and variation, as guided by the creator of the *Perry Mason* mystery novels: Erle Stanley Gardner.

Thomas Schatz notes in his work on the genres of Hollywood that the producers of a formula must constantly "vary and reinvent" the formula while not forsaking the combination of key elements that made the formula popular in the first place (36). The *Perry Mason* formula can be usefully contrasted with two other representations of the TV detective genre, *Columbo* and *The Rockford Files*. Those programs indicate the base of the genre but also show how *Perry Mason* is unique.

PERRY MASON AS FORMULA TELEVISION

Perry Mason was formulaic in the sense that the plots of the series remain true to a pattern set up in the first episode—a pattern that, by the series' end, 270 episodes later, is still intact. Perhaps this is because its literary source was already a formulaic fiction. In fact, it was the very success of the literary stories that posed a problem for the producers of the television series: how to inject "freshness" into the series as the audience became familiar with the formula.

The requirements of formula and variation in *Perry Mason* give rise to the series' distinctive narrative structure. Each episode actually comprises not one but two narrative "movements." The French critic Pierre Macherey identifies these two separate movements as being one that "establishes the mystery while the other dispels it" (34). Initiating the plot, the first movement presents "new" characters—some who may die, some who may become clients of Mason (Raymond Burr), and some who may even commit a murder or two. It is in this movement that a "problem" is stated as a crime is committed. This movement finds the most variation from episode to episode yet has its own level of necessary formulaic elements. The second narrative movement presents Mason with a client who claims innocence and compels Mason and his team to "solve" the crime. It is in this movement that the formula finds its least variation. Both movements must coexist for the story to work. The formula follows this premise: What if an innocent man/woman, who has every reason in the world to commit a murder and has little more than a flimsy alibi, is implicated and arrested for that murder and gets attorney Perry Mason to defend him/her? Taking these elements as a springboard, the show proceeds in a trajectory toward the climactic hearing or trial, where the actual murderer is revealed.

Gardner was well aware of the necessity of invention to complement the conventions of the formula, and it is he to whom creative authority could easily be attributed. Horace Newcomb and Robert Alley argue that television is a producer's medium, where individual television producers or executive producers serve as the guiding force behind a series in that they hire and control the line-producers, writers, directors, and "below-the-line" craftsmen involved in each individual episode (10). According to production records, Gardner essentially served as a co-executive producer. Besides approving the casting of the series regulars, Gardner reviewed every draft of every proposed episode as often as requested until it was changed to his liking. A *Perry Mason* episode would originate with the writing of the script, sometimes as an adaptation of one of the eighty-five Perry Mason novels and novelettes, at other times as an original idea provided by the scriptwriter. Gardner usually suggested changes that involved conforming the courtroom scenes to proper legal procedure before going before the cameras (Davidson 2), yet, just as often, Gardner would request a change in the plotting.

In each case where Gardner criticized an episode, he offered suggestions or variations in the formula. A series of odd episodes that appeared late in the sixth season illustrate how Gardner and the producers exploited the formula. When the star Raymond Burr hurt his back and was out for several episodes, instead of rerunning earlier exploits, the producers used the *Perry Mason* formula and brought in four "guest" defense attorneys: Bette Davis as the widowed partner who is left to manage "Doyle & Doyle, Attorneys at Law"; Michael Rennie as a noted law professor; Hugh O'Brian as a lawyer who defends a spy; and Walter Pidgeon as a corporate lawyer. Davis accepted the producer's offer without even looking at the script; in an interview before the episode was aired, she said that reviewing a script "wasn't necessary . . . it's a formula show, and I knew the formula" ("Bette for Burr" 80).

Proving the point, her appearance as the defense attorney in "The Case of Constant Doyle" does not disrupt the flow of the series. In the climactic courtroom scene—shot with the same cinematic look as any other *Perry Mason* episode, edited to intercut the guilty parties in the courtroom sweating as Davis explains the steps the murderer took to commit the crime—the defense attorney is not Mason but an outsider, a variation. Though the real murderer cracks up under Davis's questioning and the scene cries out for Burr to cast his dark, steely eyes upon the hapless confessor, the episode's formula stays intact—only the terms of the variation are widened a bit. Although these non-Mason episodes are failures as possible series spin-offs of *Perry Mason*, as attempts at reinvention of the formula they illustrate clearly that the cooperative strength of the formula/variation narrative structure works.

In early April of 1966, "The Case of the Final Fade-Out," the last script for the series, was written by the story editors, Ernest Frankel and Orville H. Hampton. In his critique Gardner admitted that though the script had "problems"—such as Burger going to trial without a case against Mason's client—he suggested only minor changes to the legal aspects and the general probability of the story. "This is going to be a very weak script from the standpoint of probability, but the whole plot is wacky anyway."

Story editors Frankel and Hampton had picked a young writer to be the killer—who kills because his story idea was stolen by the victim. The irony is amusing since the episode reveals much of the philosophy behind the formation of the series. Ideas, as Gardner's notes and letters suggest, were becoming hard to get—especially fresh ones. Would the producers and network kill for a new way to reinvent the formula? Ultimately, they did. Kill the series, that is. Even with its "wacky" plot, its heavily self-referential narrative, its inclusion of cameos by all the staff and crew, with Gardner himself playing the judge, the last episode continued to follow the *Perry Mason* formula.

PERRY MASON AS GENRE TELEVISION

One way of understanding the formula of any television series the size of *Perry Mason*—271 hour-long episodes—is in terms of the larger group or its genre. In television production within any particular context, especially the detective genre, a balance is necessary between the familiar and the unusual that keeps audiences interested. Jane Feuer writes that genre study provides "a field in which the force of individual creativity could play itself out" (117). In *Perry Mason* the individual creativity of Gardner and the others who worked on the production plays itself out successfully within the genre of detective television. In other programs in the detective genre, the detector can be an amateur such as the lawyer Mason in *Perry Mason*. Usually, however, the detective is professionally suited for the job, as with private investigator Jim Rockford in *The Rockford Files* and Lieutenant Philip Columbo in *Columbo*. Each of these latter series owes a debt to *Perry Mason* in two ways: *Perry Mason*, as one of the earliest detective programs, showed that a formula could be sustained through a multiple-year run and that variation from episode to episode keeps the audience interested enough to tune in each week.

Columbo aired on NBC from 1971 to 1977, with Peter Falk as the shabby, bumbling, cigar-smoking detective, and was as rigid as *Perry Mason* in its formula. Much like *Mason*, each episode would begin without the title character in the first scenes. Since the audience is privy to an elaborately staged murder and is told who "did it" in the beginning, the enigma of the series is not "who did it?" but "how will Columbo solve the crime?" The detection becomes a game for the audience to determine how Columbo, methodically, will figure out who the murderer is.

The Columbo formula is an inverted reflection of *Perry Mason*, not only in its formula but in its main character. Mason cuts a sophisticated and tailored figure, but Columbo, with his rumpled coat, beaten car, and bumbling air, evokes contempt from the individuals he is questioning—especially the killer. The lieutenant asks questions that seem to have no bearing on the case ("Tell me, offhand, how much does a place like this go for—in rent, I mean?"). And he always caps off each seemingly aimless streak of questioning with a final, direct, and possibly incriminating question, which is keyed to throw off the suspect. Here the formula is as solid and true as *Perry Mason*'s. Moreover, *Columbo* also relies on two movements to create an adequate formula/variation narrative structure. As in *Perry Mason*, most of the variation comes in the introduction of the killer, the victim, the motives, and the actual commission of the crime—the "problem" movement. The second, or "solution" movement, is more routine.

An alternate example is *The Rockford Files*, which aired on NBC between 1974 and 1980. Jim Rockford (James Garner), an ex-convict who is now a private investigator, lives and works out of his trailer on Malibu Beach and takes cases that the police have closed. Each episode begins with the phone ringing at Rockford's trailer, the answering machine going off, and messages being exchanged. The exchange is different every episode and lacks connection to the episode that follows. It serves as a cue that Rockford may miss a few cases, may not get his client off, and may not even have an innocent client to work for. And because the message changes, the audience should look for something different in each episode. This is not to say that each episode is free-form or travels from genre to genre as the wind might blow it. Instead, working within the detective genre, *Rockford* manages to incorporate a high degree of variation from which to tell the story. Rockford gets a client (an outsider or perhaps one of the cast regulars) who cannot or will not rely on the police. Rockford will use one of his many fake names, identifications, and voices to get his client out of a jam. He will get into a jam himself, and if set upon by hoods, bodyguards or other menacing obstacles, Rockford will recognize his limitations and either fight back or back off (Meyers 214). He will lose something by the end of the episode—either his fee or his pride—but his client will have done well generally by having found a place in a "Rockford file." The "solution" movement is less rigid so that it will allow for the "problem" movement, here the "case" itself, to become primary to each episode and to contain much more variation of formula. The double-movement notion, applied to *The Rockford Files*, suggests that the "solution" movement is not as rigid as in *Perry Mason* or *Columbo*, but it is present.

While it can be argued that the repeated formula of *Perry Mason* emanates from being set within the legal profession, I would contend that its perceived rigidity stems from its function as a combination of detective story *and* courtroom drama. The detective genre contains highly structured and therefore standardized formulas. It can also be argued that no other genre is as unvarying in its practices as the detective genre (perhaps because the genre relies less on the development of characters and more on the "puzzle"); and since *Mason*'s control of the narrative begins with the opening gavel, the courtroom location forces a secondary layer of formula onto the primary one of the detective story.

This may not be all that is going on in the *Perry Mason* formula, however. The common thread that links each episode to the characters, to the actors, and to the production company is the original creator, Gardner. David Bordwell ct al. identify "four senses of authorship," and one of these, the author as trademark, is most pertinent to *Perry Mason* production. Gardner's presence through all stages of the production governs the shape and scope of the formula, whether in his capacity as script consultant or as the original author of adapted works or in the presence of his name in the title sequence, and allows for the hypothesis that Gardner created any particular episode to which his name is attached (Bordwell et al. 78). It is the repetitive *Perry Mason* formula that connects the individual episodes to one another, and it is primarily the insertion of variation into the formula that differentiates one episode from another.

Erle Stanley Gardner built into each of his Perry Mason novels and—through his Paisano Productions—into the *Perry Mason* television episodes a two-movement narrative structure that allowed for variation to complement formula. This relationship is key to the success of the series in both its original and syndicated runs. Gardner clearly valued the internal structure, the basic formula. "Tell a kid the story of the 'Three Bears,'" Gardner once said, "and the child wants to hear it over and over again. Try to change it and the kid has a fit" (Hughes 250). To demonstrate further the durability of that formula, in December 1985, fifteen years after Gardner's death and nearly twenty years after "The Case of the Final Fade-Out," *Perry Mason Returns*, a two-hour telefilm, brought Mason and secretary Della Street (Barbara Hale) back to the courtroom for a highly successful revival. One of the later installments, entitled *Perry Mason and the Case of the Defiant Daughter*, earned the highest ratings in its time slot and did so against the highly publicized season premiere of *Twin Peaks* (ABC) and the Dean Koontz thriller *The Face of Fear* (CBS). Clearly the audience has not lost its taste for the formula that is *Perry Mason*. The variations of the formula are important to identify episodes as individual narratives and as part of a series; the formula itself, furthermore, serves to distinguish one series from another, but it also serves to identify a series as part of a genre. Under Gardner's influence, *Perry Mason*—with its particular narrative structure—was a model for creative variety within the formulas of the detective genre. Done to death? Never.

REFERENCES

"Bette for Burr." *Newsweek*, January 28, 1963, 80.
Bordwell, David, Janet Staiger, and Kristin Thompson. *The Classical Hollywood Cinema: Film Style and Mode of Production to 1960.* New York: Columbia University Press, 1985.
"The Case of Constant Doyle." Dir. Allan H. Miner. Written by Jackson Gillis. *Perry Mason*. CBS. January 31, 1963.
"The Case of the Final Fade-Out." Dir. Jesse Hibbs. Written by Ernest Frankel and Orville H. Hampton. *Perry Mason*. CBS. May 22, 1966.
"The Case of the Howling Dog." Dir. William D. Russell. Story by Erle Stanley Gardner. Adaptation by Seelig Lester. *Perry Mason*. CBS. April 11, 1959.
"The Case of the Libelous Locket." Dir. Arthur Marks. Written by Jonathan Latimer.

Perry Mason. CBS. February 7, 1963.

"The Case of the Surplus Suitor." Dir. Jesse Hibbs. Written by Robert C. Dennis. *Perry Mason*. CBS. February 28, 1963.

"The Case of the Two-Faced Turnabout." Dir. Arthur Marks. Written by Samuel Newman. *Perry Mason*. CBS. February 14, 1963.

Davidson, Jim. "Interview with Arthur Marks." *National Association for the Advancement of Perry Mason* 20 (March 1988).

Erle Stanley Gardner Papers. Harry Ransom Humanities Research Center, University of Texas, Austin.

Feuer, Jane. "Genre Study and Television." In *Channels of Discourse: Television and Contemporary Discourse*, edited by Robert C. Allen. Chapel Hill: University of North Carolina, 1987.

Gardner, Erle Stanley. *The Case of the Howling Dog*. New York: William Morrow, 1934. Reprint. New York: Ballantine, 1984.

Hughes, Dorothy B. *Erle Stanley Gardner: The Case of the Real Perry Mason, a Biography*. New York: William Morrow, 1978.

Kaminsky, Stuart M., and Mahan, Jeffrey H. *American Television Genres*. Chicago: Nelson-Hall, 1985.

Macherey, Pierre. *A Theory of Literary Production*, translated by Geoffrey Wall. London: Routledge and Kegan Paul, 1978.

Meyers, Richard. *TV Detectives*. San Diego, CA: A. S. Barnes, 1981.

Newcomb, Horace. *TV: The Most Popular Art*. Garden City, NY: Anchor, 1974.

Newcomb, Horace, and Alley, Robert S. *The Producer's Medium: Conversations with Creators of American TV*. New York: Oxford University Press, 1983.

Perry Mason and the Case of the Defiant Daughter. Dir. Christian Nyby II. KXAN, Austin. September 30, 1990.

Perry Mason Returns. Dir. Ron Satlof. KXAN, Austin. December 1, 1985.

The Rockford Files. Produced by Dean Hargrove. NBC televison series. 1974-1980.

Schatz, Thomas. *Hollywood Genres: Formulas, Filmmaking and the Studio System*. New York: Random House, 1981.

Index

About the Editors and Contributors

DIANA ARBIN BEN-MERRE is an associate professor at New College, Hofstra University, where she directs the writing program. She has written about Joyce and Yeats and co-edited *James Joyce and His Contemporaries*. Her poems have appeared in the *West Hills Review* and the *Irish Literary Supplement*.

J. DENNIS BOUNDS is an assistant professor of cinema-television studies in the College of Communication and the Arts at Regent University, Virginia Beach, Virginia. His entries on *Perry Mason*, Raymond Burr, and *Columbo* are due to appear in *The Encyclopedia of Television*. His book *Perry Mason: Authorship and Reproduction of a Popular Hero* is forthcoming from Greenwood Press.

JEROME H. DELAMATER is a professor of communication at Hofstra University, where he teaches courses in film studies and production. A specialist in the films of Gene Kelly, he is the author of *Dance in the Hollywood Musical* and has also written articles about the musical for the *International Encyclopedia of Dance* and about the Western for the *BFI Companion to the Western*.

GEORGE GRELLA is a professor of English and film studies and a former director of the film studies program at the University of Rochester where he teaches American literature, modern English literature, and film. He has published a great many articles and essays on detective fiction, spy fiction, and crime novels, as well as on many individual writers in the field; he also writes about other areas of popular culture and literature, including baseball and cinema.

DAVID W. MADDEN is a professor of American and Irish literatures at California State University, Sacramento. He has written two books—*Understanding Paul West* (1993) and *Critical Essays on Thomas Berger* (1995)—as well as numerous articles on a variety of subjects. He teaches a course and also has published articles on detective writers such as Thomas Berger, Jerome Charyn, Raymond Chandler, James Crumley, and Patrick McGinley.

JAMES MAXFIELD is a professor of English at Whitman College. He is the author of *The Fatal Woman: Male Anxiety in American Film Noir, 1941–1991* and has written numerous articles on both contemporary fiction and narrative film.

RUTH PRIGOZY is a professor of English at Hofstra University, where she teaches courses in American literature and film studies. She has published many articles on F. Scott Fitzgerald, as well as on Hemingway and Salinger, and on such filmmakers as Wilder, DeSica, and Griffith. She has edited Fitzgerald's *This Side of Paradise* and *The Great Gatsby*.

KATHERINE M. RESTAINO is the academic dean and the chief administrator of the Englewood Cliffs campus of Saint Peter's College. She has contributed essays for all the editions of *Twentieth Century Crime and Mystery Writers*; essays on W. J. Burley, Celia Fremlin, and Lionel Black are forthcoming in the *Dictionary of Literary Biography* series on British Mystery and Thriller Writers and on celebrities in crime and the witness for the *Oxford Companion to Crime and Mystery Writing*.

MERI-JANE ROCHELSON, an associate professor of English at Florida International University, is co-editor with Nikki Lee Manos of *Transforming Genres: New Approaches to British Fiction of the 1890s* (1994). The author of numerous articles and conference papers on Israel Zangwill and on George Eliot, she is currently at work on a new edition of Zangwill's *Children of the Ghetto* and on a larger study of Zangwill as a turn-of-the-century literary figure.

TIMOTHY SHUKER-HAINES recently received his Ph.D. in American Culture from the University of Michigan. He has presented papers on topics in twentieth-century American popular culture and is currently teaching history at an independent high school.

GARY P. STORHOFF is an associate professor of English at the University of Connecticut at Stamford, where he teaches American and African-American Literature. He has published on several authors. He is currently writing two books, one on Chester Himes and the other on depictions of the family in American literature.

JAMES O. TATE is a professor of English at Dowling College in Oakdale, New York. Professor Tate was educated at Swarthmore College and Columbia University. Among his publications are articles and essays on Flannery O'Connor, Raymond Chandler, Gavin Lyall, Walker Percy, Allen Tate, and Thomas Pynchon.

MARTHA M. UMPHREY is currently an assistant professor in the Department of Law, Jurisprudence, and Social Thought at Amherst College. She is also currently working on a cultural/legal study of the trials of Harry Thaw for the murder of Stanford White (the first "trial of the century"), entitled *Ragtime Crime: Sex and Excess in the Trials of Mad Harry Thaw*.

STEVEN WEISENBURGER is a professor of English at the University of Kentucky. He is the author of numerous articles on modern American fiction and of two books: *Fables of Subversion: Satire and the American Novel, 1930–1980* (1995), and *A Gravity's Rainbow Companion: Sources and Contexts for Pynchon's Novel* (1988).

JAN WHITT is an assistant professor in the School of Journalism and Mass Communication at the University of Colorado at Boulder. Having begun her journalism career as a reporter and editor for a newspaper and an alumni magazine in Texas, she now is working on a book about the history of women's pages. Her book *Allegory and the Modern Southern Novel* was published in 1994.

ISBN 0-313-30463-7

HARDCOVER BAR CODE